Rethinking Case Study Research

Comparative case studies are an effective qualitative tool for researching the impact of policy and practice in various fields of social research, including education. Developed in response to the inadequacy of traditional case study approaches, comparative case studies are highly effective because of their ability to synthesize information across time and space. In *Rethinking Case Study Research: A Comparative Approach*, the authors describe, explain, and illustrate the horizontal, vertical, and transversal axes of comparative case studies in order to help readers develop their own comparative case study research designs. In six concise chapters, two experts employ geographically distinct case studies—from Tanzania to Guatemala to the U.S.—to show how this innovative approach applies to the operation of policy and practice across multiple social fields. With examples and activities from anthropology, development studies, and policy studies, this volume is written for researchers, especially graduate students, in the fields of education and the interpretive social sciences.

Lesley Bartlett is Professor in the Department of Educational Policy Studies and a faculty affiliate with the Department of Anthropology and the Department of Curriculum and Instruction at the University of Wisconsin-Madison, USA.

Frances Vavrus is Professor in the Department of Organizational Leadership, Policy, and Development and a faculty affiliate at the Interdisciplinary Center for the Study of Global Change at the University of Minnesota, USA.

Rethinking Case Study Research
A Comparative Approach

Lesley Bartlett
and Frances Vavrus

Routledge
Taylor & Francis Group

NEW YORK AND LONDON

First published 2017
by Routledge
711 Third Avenue, New York, NY 10017

and by Routledge
2 Park Square, Milton Park, Abingdon, Oxon OX14 4RN

Routledge is an imprint of the Taylor & Francis Group, an informa business

Library of Congress Cataloging in Publication Data
Names: Bartlett, Lesley, author. | Vavrus, Frances Katherine, author.
Title: Rethinking case study research : a comparative approach /
Lesley Bartlett and Frances Vavrus.
Description: New York : Routledge, 2017.
Identifiers: LCCN 2016039050| ISBN 9781138939516 (hardback) |
ISBN 9781138939523 (pbk.) | ISBN 9781315674889 (e-book)
Subjects: LCSH: Case method. | Comparative education.
Classification: LCC LB1029.C37 B38 2017 | DDC 371.39—dc23
LC record available at https://lccn.loc.gov/2016039050

ISBN: 978-1-138-93951-6 (hbk)
ISBN: 978-1-138-93952-3 (pbk)
ISBN: 978-1-315-67488-9 (ebk)

Typeset in Goudy
by Book Now Ltd, London

Contents

Acknowledgments

Books are social accomplishments: They result from engaging the ideas of a long line of authors who precede us; the support provided by funders, publishers, and editorial staff; trying and failing and trying again with new methods ideas in conjunction with our students; a lot of interactions with colleagues across the years; and of course the joy of dialogic thinking with a co-author.

Lesley gratefully acknowledges the generous support of the Spencer Foundation, whose Midcareer Fellowship made much of her writing for the book possible, and Frances extends her thanks to the Fulbright Scholars Program and the University of Minnesota's McKnight Presidential Fellows program for its support of the Tanzania research discussed in Chapter 5. We both want to recognize the funders who made possible the Tanzania research discussed elsewhere in the book. They include AfricAid, the Open Society Foundations, the TAG Foundation, and the Teachers College Provost Investment Fund.

We wish to thank the students in our research methods classes, past and present, for their questions as we developed the material in this book; we also want to acknowledge, for the inspiration they provided, the former students who wrote the chapters in the first book, including Audrey Bryan, Ameena Ghaffar Kucher, Maria Hantzopolous, Jill Koyama, Rosemary Max, Mary Mendenhall, Tonya Muro, Janet Shriberg, Aleesha Taylor, Laura Valdiviezo, Moira Wilkinson, and Zeena Zakharia. Since publishing that book, we have had the pleasure of meeting or working with a number of people who have taken the ideas of comparative case studies in new directions. We wish to particularly acknowledge Martina Arnal, Maria Jose Bermeo, Karen Bryner, Ferdinand Chipindi, Paulo da Silva, Scott Freeman, Regina Fuller, Meg Gardinier, Toni Cela Hamm, Christina Kwauk, Dina Lopez, Gabrielle Oliveira, Diana Rodriguez Gomez, Laura Scheiber, Sarah Smith, Matthew Thomas, Lori Ungemah, Tamara Webb, and Jaime Usma Wilches.

We also thank colleagues who have provided stimulating conversations around research methods and who have suggested readings, including Monisha Bajaj, Michelle Bellino, Joan DeJaeghere, Peter Demerath, Jonathon Fairhead, Gerry Fry, Ofelia García, Meg Gardinier, Nancy Kendall, Adam Nelson,

Aaron Pallas, Oren Pizmony-Levy, Erica Simmons, Gita Steiner-Khamsi, Herve Varenne, Bethany Wilinski, Rachelle Winkle-Wagner, the Qualitative Methods group at UW-Madison and their Speaker's Series, and the faculty of Mwenge Catholic University.

Finally, we would like to thank our families for their patience with us when our investments in this book robbed time from other activities. Lesley is grateful for the writing time, snacks, and dance party study breaks provided by Brian, Owen, and Lila. Frances expresses her gratitude to Gus, Oscar, and Tim Leinbach, and she hopes the young scholars in the family may one day use this book for their own research.

1 Follow the Inquiry

An Introduction

In his 2004 article "What is a case study and what is it good for?," political scientist John Gerring noted that, though case studies continue to be used widely, researchers "have difficulty articulating what it is that they are doing, methodologically speaking. *The case study survives in a curious methodological limbo*" (p. 341, emphasis ours). In this book, we respond to that widespread methodological limbo by introducing a promising approach for critical, comparative research—the comparative case study approach—that attends simultaneously to global, national, and local dimensions of case-based research. We contend that new approaches are necessitated by conceptual shifts in the social sciences, specifically in relation to culture, context, space, place, and comparison itself.

The comparative case study approach—which we will refer to by the acronym CCS throughout this book—is particularly well-suited to social research about practice and policy. By practice, we mean to signal studies that consider how social actors, with diverse motives, intentions, and levels of influence, work in tandem with and/or in response to social forces to routinely produce the social and cultural worlds in which they live (Ortner, 1984; see also Giddens, 1984; Bourdieu, 1977; de Certeau, 1984). Some practices are widely shared, such as assessing children's academic competence through written examinations; others, such as the marking of a marriage or a death, can be quite specific to a place and time. Practices are never isolated. Social actors adopt and develop practices in relation to other groups—sometimes to distinguish themselves, and sometimes to declare (or aspire to) group membership. Further, practices always develop in relation to broader political, social, cultural, and economic environments.

This conceptualization of practice extends to our approach to policy, an area of scholarship that is increasingly recognized as vital to understanding how contemporary social life is regulated and governed. It is essential to note from the outset that the CCS approach engages an expansive definition of "policy as practice" (Shore & Wright, 1997; Levinson & Sutton, 2001). While some approaches to policy studies adopt an instrumentalist stance to investigate 'what works,' a sociocultural approach understands policy as a deeply political process of cultural production engaged in and shaped by social actors in disparate locations who exert incongruent amounts of influence over the design, implementation, and evaluation of policy. These actors differ in their authority to "(1) define what is problematic; (2) shape interpretations and means of how problems should be resolved; and (3) determine to what vision of the future change efforts should be directed" (Hamann & Rosen, 2011, p. 462). These three points highlight how sociocultural approaches to policy-as-practice attend to the political contestations that shape the policy cycle.

Although theoretical advances have been made by scholars who conceptualize policy as a set of social practices of actors across locations, methodological clarity as to how one might explore the formation and appropriation of policies across multiple sites and scales has heretofore been limited. Further, there is heightened attention today to the influence of non-governmental actors in the formation of state and national policy, from Wall Street (Ho, 2009) and the American Legislative Exchange Council (ALEC)—the "public-private partnership" between legislators and corporations responsible for controversial laws across many states (Scola, 2012)—to social movements like the Black Lives Matter campaign and international organizations that run the gamut from Amnesty International to the World Bank (Goldman, 2006). However, it has proven challenging for many researchers to conduct analyses of policy and practice at these scales while also attending to how policies unfold in particular communities. The CCS approach that we offer in this book argues for multi-scalar research to address these challenges.

A sociocultural lens for looking at policy as practice requires attention to both policy formation and policy implementation as cultural and social processes. Policy formation results in "a normative cultural discourse with positive and negative sanctions, that is, a set of statements about how things should or must be done, with corresponding inducements or punishments" (Levinson, Sutton, & Winstead, 2009, p. 770); in other words, policy profoundly shapes our view of the world, how different actors should behave in it, and what the consequences should be if rules are not followed. Yet formal, written policies encode selective representations of social groups and exclude many of their struggles in ways that have serious consequences regarding who is held responsible for social ills, such as mass incarceration or low levels of literacy; policy authorizes certain social actors to define problems and solutions, thereby shaping public discourses in ways that often prove stubbornly resistant to change (Ball, 1994). Policy implementation occurs through a complex process of *appropriation*, during which social actors interpret and selectively implement policies, thereby adapting ideas and discourses developed in a different place and potentially at a different historical moment and harnessing them for their own purposes. This notion of policy appropriation as cultural and social production is founded upon practice theory (e.g., Bourdieu, 1977, 1990), which is known for arguing against structure/agency dichotomies in favor of attention to the moment when both are mutually constituted through social practice (Levinson et al., 2009). Thus, rather than reproducing a structure/agency divide, as some have argued (Robertson, 2012), the CCS approach we are proposing examines how structures are culturally produced in what anthropologist Anna Tsing called the "friction" of social practice (Tsing, 2005).

In our initial conceptualization, we dubbed this approach a "vertical case study," and the term has gained traction in our principal field of comparative education (Vavrus & Bartlett, 2006, 2009, 2013; Bartlett & Vavrus, 2014). However, our decade of reflection and writing has made clear the value of identifying three axes, not only one, in comparative research—the vertical, the horizontal, and the transversal. What we aim for in renaming this approach is akin to what anthropologist Ulf Hannerz dubbed "studying through" (2006, p. 24). The horizontal axis compares how similar policies unfold in *distinct locations* that are *socially produced* (Massey, 2005) and *"complexly connected"* (Tsing, 2005, p. 6). The vertical axis insists on simultaneous attention *to and across scales* (see also Bray & Thomas, 1995; Nespor, 2004, 1997). The transversal comparison *historically* situates the processes or relations under consideration. Each of these axes is developed in depth and illustrated with examples in subsequent chapters. We seek to show how social research, including but not limited to policy research, would benefit from attention across these three axes.

An extended example of the axes of the CCS approach may be helpful at this early juncture. Figure 1.1 represents a study we conducted with American and Tanzanian colleagues regarding the impact on Tanzanian teachers' practice of the global push toward learner-centered pedagogy (LCP), an approach to teaching in which students are actively engaged in meaningful and constructive learning in the classroom as opposed to listening to lectures and memorizing factual information (Vavrus & Bartlett, 2013). During the past few decades, LCP has been heavily promoted by international education and

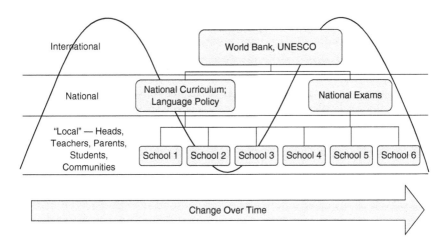

Figure 1.1 Comparative Case Study Approach to Learner-Centered Pedagogy in Tanzania.

development organizations for various reasons, including its assumed benefits for cognitive growth, self-efficacy and empowerment, and democratization and the development of civil society (Schweisfurth, 2013). Since the mid 2000s, it has also been partially adopted by the Tanzanian government in its education policies and curricula.

Illustrating the transversal axis, our study examined the ways in which LCP, a specific approach to teaching and learning popularized in the temporal and cultural context of the United States and the UK in the 1970s (Cuban, 1993; Ravitch, 1983), has been taken up, simplified, and spread globally. In that process, learner-centered pedagogy diffused very particular understandings of teaching and learning that rely upon culturally-specific notions of individualism, competition, cooperation, and authority and presume certain material conditions in schools and classrooms (see also Vavrus & Bartlett, 2012). Emphasizing change over time, we examined how the government of Tanzania has incorporated this perspective on teaching and learning into its education policies over the past 50 years. We used discourse analysis (discussed further in Chapter 4) to trace the gradual incorporation of global ways of framing learning in national educational policies, beginning in the *Education for All* era of the 1990s.

A careful vertical analysis across scales is also important to the type of case study approach we propose. We emphasize the importance of examining policy formation and appropriation across micro-, meso-, and macro-levels. In *Teaching in Tension*, we documented consequential tensions that influenced the appropriation of learner-centered pedagogy. External donor funding supported Tanzanian curricular projects, which incorporated heavy doses of LCP (Bartlett & Vavrus, 2014). Around this time, donors, and especially the World Bank, also emphasized the importance of rigorous, standardized testing to measure educational quality and hold teachers accountable, leading to a significant contradiction when assessment specialists within the National Examination Council of Tanzania continued to devise high-stakes exams that captured rote memorization more than critical thinking. Because the tests had serious consequences for student advancement to secondary school and college, for teachers who may receive "motivation" money if their students perform well, and for schools (especially private schools) whose existence may depend on the high scores that attract new families and their tuition fees, the tests paradoxically encouraged methods that emphasize the memorization of factual information rather than learner-centered pedagogical approaches. This tendency was compounded by the breadth of the exams, which cover four years of information for seven or more subjects, making the acquisition of both core knowledge and higher-order thinking skills a great challenge. Thus, the curricular and assessment arms of the Ministry of Education and Vocational Training were in conflict, and actors located in international and national organizations had a great influence over the policies and curricular materials available to educators.

The larger study also made use of horizontal comparisons across six high schools in two adjacent regions in Tanzania to demonstrate the significant impact of transnational institutions and social movements on the material conditions of local schools and on the organizational dynamics within them. For instance, teachers at the school funded by an American non-profit organization enjoyed extensive professional development in learner-centered pedagogy, a life skills program for students, a sizable library with materials for developing inquiry-based projects, and relative material wealth as reflected in the availability of books, handouts, paper, photocopiers, and Internet access. These factors influenced the shape and tenor of the appropriation of LCP at that school, as observed by the research team and reported by its teachers. In contrast, the Catholic and Anglican schools, affiliated with powerful and quite hierarchical transnational institutions, presented a markedly different context within which to develop the more egalitarian relations between teachers and students that are implicit in LCP. For example, one teacher at a Catholic school complained that there were constraints on teachers organizing debates among students on topics of concern and interest to students, such as prostitution or HIV/AIDS. In religiously-affiliated schools, teachers' appropriations of the educational policies promoted by international institutions and embedded in national curricula were heavily influenced by religious notions of propriety, including gender norms.

More broadly, the horizontal comparison across these six high schools demonstrated how different material and ideological contexts affected the appropriation of learner-centered pedagogy within one country. According to the Tanzanian teachers who participated in the study, LCP is simply more difficult to implement in schools with overcrowded classrooms, few books to share among many students, limited poster board for making teaching aids, and even notebook paper to enhance group or pair work (Vavrus & Bartlett, 2013).

Finally, a horizontal comparison reminds us that policy is also made locally, and that teachers are key actors in educational policy appropriation: they interpret, negotiate, and revise policies on assessment, curriculum content, pedagogical methods, and language of instruction in the classroom (see, e.g., Menken & García, 2010). Our study, for instance, compared how teachers at six secondary schools struggled to implement a competency-based curriculum when the high-stakes, national exams continued to emphasize the recall of facts. Further, the project documented how teachers creatively enacted language policy, influenced by their own biographies as language learners as well as the social and material conditions in their schools and surrounding communities. Officially, at the time, secondary school teachers were required to teach and assess in English; however, this policy interfered with the implementation of learner-centered pedagogy because the latter demands greater English oral fluency in the language than many students (and quite a few teachers) possess (see Webb & Mkongo, 2013). Teachers commented frequently on the contradictory pressures created for them by the language, curricular, and assessment policies.

We hope it is clear from this example that the three axes of a comparative case study are mutually imbricated. For example, in comparing horizontally across schools and the teachers in them, we considered individual teachers' biographies; in comparing vertically, we looked at how the relationship between international donors and the Tanzanian state differentially affected local schools; and, running through the entire project was the transversal axis of learner-centered pedagogy and how its growing prominence in Tanzanian education policy over time has shaped teachers' biographies and has been shaped by donor–state relationships. Though we extricate the axes in subsequent chapters for purposes of explaining and illustrating them, it is essential to note the extent to which they can and do overlap.

The main objective of this book, then, is to describe, explain, and illustrate the horizontal, vertical, and transversal axes of comparative case studies with examples and activities to help researchers, especially graduate students, develop their own CCS research designs. Throughout the book, we have included exercises aimed at helping researchers think about how to use comparative case studies in their own projects by working incrementally to develop a research topic and study design. The volume is directed at researchers in any of the interpretive social sciences; however, our joint expertise lies in the field of education, and our areas of specialization are in anthropology, development studies, and policy studies. While the examples provided draw primarily from these fields, we believe the utility of this book extends to anyone studying how policy and practice operate across multiple social fields and unfold over time.

Exercise 1.1 Analyze a Case Study

Case study is a widely used methodology in many fields, including education, nursing, political science, and sociology. You have probably read many case studies, but you may not have stopped to analyze them methodologically.

- Find a case study in your field. How did the author define and/or delimit the case? What research methods did the author engage, such as interviewing, observation, or surveying? What are the strengths and weaknesses of this study in terms of its ability to convince you of the specificity of the case *and* its significance for understanding a larger social phenomenon? What is your sense of how this case study compares to others in your field?
- Find a *comparative* case study in your field. This may be more difficult because, as we discuss in Chapter 2, some case study scholars eschew comparison. If you did find one, what did the author compare and how was this done? What are the strengths and weaknesses of this study in relation to the single-case study you reviewed? What is your sense of how it compares to other comparative case studies in your field?

We consider the CCS approach to be a *heuristic*. Derived from a Greek word that means "to discover," *heuristic* can be defined as method that comes from experience and aids in the process of discovery or problem-solving. It is not a recipe or a set of rules. Rather, the CCS approach is, first and foremost, a reminder of *how much we might achieve through comparison*. Comparing and contrasting are essential analytical moves, and yet they are often rejected by qualitative case study researchers who feel that their commitment to context precludes comparison. We believe this oversight is a major missed opportunity because case study research could benefit immensely from incorporating comparison into study designs and data analysis. Indeed, justifying the significance of a study often requires that one compare the specific case to other, similar circumstances. In some instances, including a comparison may entail thinking about the work in *phases*, like a sequential mixed methods design. For instance, one might conduct three comparative case studies in the first month of fieldwork to see general relationships before focusing on one of the cases for a more detailed, processual look, or (alternately) one might complete an ethnographic case study for a longer period to generate a theory before conducting several shorter, comparative case studies in the second phase to refine the theory by seeing what it may or may not explain in different cases. The CCS approach is also a heuristic in the sense that the three axes (horizontal, vertical, and transversal) serve to remind us of possible, fruitful directions for comparison. There may be studies that examine only two of these axes, and few studies emphasize all three equally. However, all researchers contemplating the CCS approach should ask themselves whether they are missing a significant part of the story by ignoring one axis. In developing the CCS heuristic, we assume that most readers intend to use primarily qualitative research methods, such as observation, interviewing, and discourse analysis, but we also emphasize that questionnaires or surveys can help to gain a comparative perspective.

In the process of developing the CCS heuristic in this book, we must also explain how it differs from predominant approaches to case study research in the social sciences. This issue is addressed in greater depth in Chapter 2, but suffice it to say that some of the case study literature embraces a positivist epistemology, a variable-oriented theory of causation, and social scientific notions of validity and reliability that obfuscate the very advantages of case studies. Instead, in this book we adopt what Joseph Maxwell (2013) called a *process approach* to trace *how* and *why* phenomena take place. Such questions "involve an open-ended, inductive approach to discover what these meanings and influences are and *how* they are involved in these events and activities— an inherently processual orientation" (p. 83). This stance leads us to *follow the inquiry* in an iterative, emergent research design. Further, we argue that existing approaches to case study research are frequently premised upon outdated notions of culture, context, and comparison. This volume seeks to remedy these limitations and will offer guidance to researchers—both novices and more experienced scholars—regarding the possibilities of an approach to case study research that places culture, context, comparison, and a critical understanding of power at its core.

Exercise 1.2 What Phenomena Interest You?

According to Merriam-Webster, a phenomenon is "something (such as an interesting fact or event) that can be observed and studied and that typically is unusual or difficult to understand or explain fully." We have read many dissertation proposals over the years, and the best ones have, at their core, a counter-intuitive fact or unanticipated event that the researcher wants to understand more fully. Sometimes we have asked our students, "What is your puzzle? What are you trying to figure out?" However, for first-year graduate students, this is often too big a question as it may feel like the answer has to be momentous, such as trying to find a cure for cancer or a solution to racial inequality in schools. Instead, the word *phenomenon* directs us, first, toward the 'thing' itself and then, as it comes into focus, we can ask what is odd or unexpected about it, and why and to whom it matters. So, now that you have looked at a few case studies in your field, it's time to turn to your research project:

- What are two or three "somethings" in the world that concern you that you do not fully understand?

Now we can move into a few more specific questions, which still do not have to lead to solving one of the world's great mysteries but will promote understanding of something that matters to you and to relevant others:

- How might a comparative case study help you to understand at least one of these phenomena?
- What could you learn about this phenomenon through a comparative case study that you could not learn using another approach to research? What might these alternative approaches help you to understand that a CCS might not?
- What are two or three research questions you could ask about this phenomenon that you could answer through a CCS? Keep in mind that you will need to revise these as you develop a conceptual framework and move through your research design (Maxwell, 2013).

How CCS Re-envisions Culture, Context, and Comparison

Though it draws on the tradition of case study research, the CCS method differs from traditional case study approaches in several important ways, which are further described in Chapter 2. Specifically, comparative case studies adopt a processual stance to re-envision three key concepts in case study research: culture, context, and comparison.

Culture

First, comparative case studies employ a significant reconceptualization of culture. As explained in Erickson's (2011) excellent overview of the term, "culture" has a complicated history. He noted that the "basic contrast term for 'culture' is 'nature,'" and culture "originally referred to human activity that transformed the state of nature in the physical world" (p. 25). The concept of culture was also an effort by anthropologists like Franz Boas to supplant what, at that time, were dominant, racist explanations for human differences. In its most common usage, culture refers to human activities that indicate commonality among a group of people in terms of their sense of a shared history or common rules governing social life that distinguish them more or less rigidly from other people.

By the 1960s, and increasingly in the 1970s, recognition of differences within a so-called 'culture' and the shift from a homeostatic to a conflict-based understanding of social life challenged this traditional notion of culture. Theorists sought to maintain a sense of the importance of symbolic production and meaning making; anthropologists like Clifford Geertz dedicated themselves to symbolic or interpretive anthropology, a field that attended to the role of symbols in constructing public meaning and the belief "that man [sic] is an animal suspended in webs of significance he himself has spun" (Geertz, 1973, p. 5). At the same time, Marxist anthropologists and other critical theorists emphasized attention to economic and social conditions that affect human activity and shared meaning. For example, Roseberry (1989) argued that Geertz took an idealist position, ignoring economic factors and historical processes, and treating culture as product, not process. Major sociological work propelled the notion of culture from "a set of rules" to something more akin to principles or understandings that people used to "make sense" (Garfinkel, 1984, 2002) or develop a "feel for the game" (Bourdieu, 1990). Furthermore, scholars averred that what is important is not cultural difference per se, but when and how cultural difference is made consequential—e.g., when difference is cast as deficit or disability (e.g., McDermott & Varenne, 1995).

After significant revision, some anthropologists advocated for the total rejection of the culture concept. For example, Abu-Lughod (1991) wrote a scathing critique, arguing that static, homogenous notions of culture had become as problematic as race, and just as likely to be mobilized to discriminate (e.g., through culture of poverty stereotypes) (see also Fox & King, 2002). However, others defended the term for its enduring analytical utility. For example, anthropologist Sherry Ortner (1999) concluded, "the point is not that there is no longer anything we would call 'culture,' but that interpretive analysis of social groups should be situated within and, as it were, beneath larger analyses of social and political events and processes" (p. 9).

Responding to these critiques, contemporary understandings of culture are more complex. As anthropologist Anderson-Levitt clarified, "since the 1980s many anthropologists have shifted the focus to practice or performance and hence emphasize the process of making meaning over the meanings themselves" (2012, p. 443). Today, anthropologically-informed scholarship generally treats culture as an ever-changing, active, productive process of sense-making in concert with others. To capture this sense, anthropologist Brian Street suggested that it might be best to conceptualize culture as a verb (1993). Notably, "culture does not do things to people; rather, people do things, and one important thing they do is make meaning" (Anderson-Levitt, 2012, p. 444). While groups may "claim to own culture" for strategic reasons, "not everyone inside the group necessarily shares the same beliefs and norms" (Anderson-Levitt, 2012, pp. 444–445); such moments of strategic essentialism should, themselves, be analyzed. Finally, though cultural innovation occurs locally through social interaction, these interactions need not be face-to-face and may instead be mediated by social media or other technologies, as in the cases of online communities of political activists or persons with the same illness who communicate regularly with one another (Erickson, 2011; Anderson-Levitt, 2012). These communities of practice are multiple and shift over time as new members join and older members move on. The point is that culture is not uniform; as Erickson (2011) explained:

> to be human is to be multicultural, to be engaged continually in new culturing activity, because it appears that all humans participate in multiple local communities of practice and take action opportunistically within them. Thus, within the conduct of their everyday lives, humans develop personal repertoires of practice that are multiplex and dynamically changing, rather than participating in a single, unitary cultural entity and following passively a single system of cultural rules.
>
> (p. 32)

Perhaps most importantly, contests over meaning and practice are influenced by power relations, including direct imposition and, more commonly, the cultural production of "common sense" notions of social order.

There are important implications of this shift in conceptualizations of culture for case study research. While case studies frequently include a focus on meaning, this has sometimes been conceptualized as 'discovering' the meaning of a particular term or idea among members of 'a' culture or subculture, such as the meaning of style, respect, or success for working-class youth in Detroit or hedge fund managers in New York City. In contrast to this sense of (static) culture within a (bounded) group, the understanding of culture that undergirds the CCS approach provides strong justification for the importance of examining *processes* of sense-making as they develop over time, in distinct settings, in relation to systems of power and inequality, and in increasingly interconnected conversation with actors who do not sit physically within the circle drawn around the traditional case. The CCS heuristic warns against static and essentializing notions of culture, recommends attention to cultural repertoires and contestation, and emphasizes the need to consider power relations within a single institution or community and across communities, states, and nations. It also suggests that researchers pay particular attention to language, discourse, texts, and institutions as important social and policy actors. Finally, it insists on attention to social interactions, which may or may not transpire in person. This insight begs a consideration of *context*, the second key term we consider central to CCS research.

Exercise 1.3 Culture

Spend one day documenting the number of times you hear, use, or see in print the term "culture."

- How is it being used? What are some of the problems with those uses given the concerns raised above?
- How would a more contemporary, processual use of the notion of culture that attends to power (e.g., as cultural practices or 'culture as a verb') change the conversation?
- Do the research questions you developed in the previous exercise explicitly or implicitly reference a notion of culture? If so, are you engaging a contemporary notion of culture? How might your questions use cultural analysis?

Context

The CCS heuristic draws upon a radical rethinking of context, another concept that is much-cited and yet ill-defined in case study research. In common parlance, context is often used to indicate the physical setting of people's actions. The importance exerted by context is one of the primary reasons for selecting a case study approach to research. To represent this aspect, some scholars refer to contextual or ecological validity. These terms originated in psychological studies to indicate "the extent to which the environment experienced by the subjects in a scientific investigation has the properties it is supposed or assumed to have by the experimenter" (Bronfenbrenner, 1977, p. 516). Since that time, among sociocultural scholars, the term has come to suggest the importance of maintaining the integrity of real-world situations rather than studying a phenomenon in laboratory contexts. The concept offers an implicit critique of the effort to generalize by stripping away the particular. As Geertz wrote, "No one lives in the world in general. Everyone, even the exiled, the drifting, the diasporic, or the perpetually moving, lives in some confined and limited stretch of it—'the world around here'" (1996, p. 262).

This point, we fully agree, is quite important. However, scholars continue to rely on a rather static, confined, and deterministic sense of context. No 'place' is unaffected by history and politics; any specific location is influenced by economic, political, and social processes well beyond its physical and temporal boundaries. As literacy scholars Leander and Sheehy have argued, "context … has been overdetermined in its meaning by a seemingly natural interpretation of material setting or place" (2004, p. 3). In considering digital literacies, Leander contended that multiple contexts are articulated and juxtaposed when a young person reads a 'zine online, for example, or chats with a friend from another city. The same is true in a wide array of cultural practices. Leander urged attention to "how practices produce locations" (2002, p. 3). Indeed, we argue that scholars need to consider how and why participants (re)create boundaries through social interactions across space and time.

In this vein, we contend that settings are constituted by social activities and social interactions (Duranti & Goodwin, 1992; Dyson & Genishi, 2005). Indeed, for those who draw upon activity theory, activity itself is the context—made up of actors, their objectives, their actions, and the artifacts they engage, each with their relevant histories (see, e.g., Cole, 1996; Engeström, 1987; Engeström, Miettinen, & Punamäki, 1999). In this view, context is not a container for activity; it *is* the activity. Engaging a notion of culture as strategic and symbolic "sense making," we can see activities as purposeful efforts to respond to uncertainty in how to move forward. This way of thinking about context is also enhanced by Bourdieu's concept of "field," a symbolic arena in which agents are relatively positioned based on the (arbitrary, socially constructed, and open to negotiation) rules of the field, the agent's symbolic capital, and the agent's habitus (Bourdieu & Wacquant, 1992). We also embrace the idea of "fuzzy fields," which Nadai and Maeder described as "social worlds … formed by sets of common or joint activities or concerns bound together by a network of communications," wherein "sets of actors [are] focused on a common concern and [act] on the basis of a minimal working consensus" (2005). They continued, stating that "identifying adequate sites, which add up to an ethnographic field, requires a theoretical clarification of the object of study first. Such a theoretical framework can then serve as a compass for the search of a field" (2005). That object of study is what we call the phenomenon of interest. In short, context is made; it is relational and spatial (see also Gupta & Ferguson, 1997).

Our notion of context also attends to power relations and the critical theories of place and space put forward by critical geographers and anthropologists. Doreen Massey (1991, 2005) argued explicitly against the romantic idea that a place has a single, essential identity based on a limited history of territory. In this view, place becomes a static, dead object. She critiqued this desire for fixity and boundedness:

Instead then, of thinking of places as areas with boundaries around, they can be imagined as articulated moments in networks of social relations and understandings, but where a large proportion of those relations, experiences and understandings are constructed on a far larger scale than what we happen to define for that moment as the place itself, whether that be a street, or a region or even a continent. And this in turn allows a sense of place which is extroverted, which includes a consciousness of its links with the wider world, which integrates in a positive way the global and the local.

(1991, p. 28)

So-called local contexts, she argued, are quite heterogeneous and produced from the intersection of social, economic, and cultural relations linked to various scales.

Further, rethinking the production of and interconnections across sites reveals the sociocultural production of inequality. As Gupta and Ferguson (1992) wrote, "The presumption that spaces are autonomous has enabled the power of topography to conceal successfully the topography of power" (p. 8). They asserted the importance of examining historically the processes by which local sites with different patterns of social relations came into being, rather than treating them as primordial places:

> taking a preexisting, localized 'community' as a given starting point … fails to examine sufficiently the processes (such as the structures of feeling that pervade the imagining of community) that go into the construction of space as place or locality in the first instance. In other words, instead of assuming the autonomy of the primeval community, we need to examine how it was formed *as a community* out of the interconnected space that always already existed.

(1997, p. 36; emphasis in original;
see also Appadurai, 1999)

Gupta and Ferguson interrogated the all-too-common, apolitical and ahistorical term "community," and they insisted on a historical and processual approach (see also Vavrus, 2015).

Not only are sites not autonomous—they are influenced by actions well beyond the local context and the current moment, and thus the idea of 'bounding' them, which others argue is the hallmark of case study research, is an illusion. The 'unbounding' we call for in CCS research requires attention to the processes mentioned above. It also requires attention to *scale*. Scale is often used to distinguish local, regional, national, and global levels, though critical geographers have argued forcefully against the tendency to conceptualize these as distinct and unrelated. As Bruno Latour stated, "the macro is neither 'above' nor 'below' the interactions, but *added* to them as *another* of their connections" (2005, p. 177).[1] In CCS research, one would pay close attention to how actions at different scales mutually influence one another. Middleton (2014) made this point succinctly: "To make social relations their objects of inquiry, researchers must adopt a multi-scalar focus and engage in multilevelled analysis. They must identify relations of proximity and distance, tracing relational links between near and far" (p. 18). These relations are critical to understanding how topographies of power are formed through the concatenation of multi-scalar political-economic forces that act upon the social imaginary to produce towns, neighborhoods, and villages out of previously non-demarcated space, and to bestow privileges upon some of them but not others.

This line of spatial theorizing at the global (and, in some cases, regional and national) scale has proven to be quite productive for the study of practice and policy, but it has neglected, with a few notable exceptions, the social production of space at *local* scales. As Larsen and Beech stated, "Place continues to be implicitly conceptualized as the local (or the subnational or national), the real, and the stable; and space as the global, something more abstract, futuristic, and beyond us" (2014, p. 195; see also Robertson, 2012). In her critique of the sociological literature on globalization, Oke (2009) made this point even more forcefully while discussing how place tends to be conceptualized as outside of global relations of power and how globalization is frequently theorized with little regard to context:

> While place might be the home of history and culture, power is understood as located in space. This downplays the contingent, historically constructed aspects of globalization, the agency of actors and the diversity of processes contained under the banner of globalization . . . . This leads to understanding of change as occurring outside particular contexts, allowing globalization to be understood as a singular and systemic driving power with a tendency to suggest it has a systemic logic outside such contexts.
>
> (p. 323)

One corrective to this tendency in the study of globalization is to engage in historical, multi-scalar research that engages more deeply with analysis at regional and local scales within particular nation-states, and to examine how places of power come into being under particular conditions (Taylor, Rees, Sloan, & Davies, 2013).

This reconceptualization of context using spatial theory has important implications for case study work. It encourages us to attend very carefully to the social relations and networks that constitute the most relevant context in one's research and how these relations and networks have formed and shifted over time. Context is not a primordial or autonomous place; it is constituted by social interactions, political processes, and economic developments across scales and across time. Rethinking context steers us away from "bounding" a study *a priori* and, instead, makes the project one of identifying the historical and contemporary networks of actors, institutions, and policies that produce some sense of a bounded place for specific purposes. This inversion of the case study research process has important implications for comparison.

Exercise 1.4 Context

Review your favorite book or article on research methods.

- How does the researcher discuss context? Are there elements of the author's approach that you want to avoid and, if so, why? Are there elements you wish to emulate? If so, what makes these elements useful for your project?
- How would a multi-scalar notion of context change the research design you are considering? How might it influence your research questions?
- Make a list of the places you might need to include in your study in order to address your phenomenon of interest and begin documenting how you might explore the histories of contestation, privilege, and/or marginalization that produced them as identifiable places.

Comparison

The CCS heuristic heavily emphasizes the value of comparison across space and time. As we note in Chapter 2, explicit comparison has been under-utilized in case study work and, more broadly, in qualitative research. Yet there is much to gain from comparing. It allows us to think how similar processes lead to different outcomes in some situations; how different influences lead to similar outcomes in others; and how seemingly distinct phenomena may be related to similar trends or pressures. Comparison may also allow us to better address how insights generated in one study transfer to other cases; in this way, comparison allows us to make stronger arguments for the significance of our research.

Notably, comparison means different things to different people, and exposing these differences helps to clarify our argument. At the risk of over-simplifying, we adopt Maxwell's (2013) terminology to identify two general approaches to comparison: those that are variance-oriented (and therefore tend to rely on a positivist epistemology and use quantitative methods), and those that are process-oriented (and thus tend to employ a more interpretive, constructivist, or critical epistemology and qualitative methods). Comparative case studies promote processual understandings of comparison, while many of the predominant approaches to case study research in different fields are variance-oriented.

For some fields, comparison generally means quantitative research and cross-national comparison. The dominant model of comparison in political science promotes many cases and comparison across units (e.g., national or subnational units) that are presumed, prima facia, to be the same (e.g., Snyder, 2001), and it requires the identification of hypotheses about relationships between independent and dependent variables (Landman & Robinson, 2009; see critique in Simmons & Smith, 2015). The "controlled" or "paired comparison" model, which often relies on case selection strategies that minimize or maximize differences in presumed independent and dependent variables, gives variables a central role (see, e.g., Gisselquist, 2014; Slater & Ziblatt, 2013; Tarrow, 2010). Area studies in comparative politics, which are more likely to feature qualitative research, still generally privilege comparison across nation-states and judge qualitative research by positivist notions of validity, reliability, and generalizability (Simmons & Smith, 2015). Process tracing, one of the most processual approaches in comparative politics, aims to lay out the mechanisms that connect independent and dependent variables and "document whether the sequence of events or processes within the case fits those predicted by alternative explanations of the case" (Bennett, 2008, p. 705; see also Caporaso, 2009, George & Bennett, 2004). Even advocates of "contextualized comparisons" that select cases which are "analytically parallel" and focus on complex dynamics rather than attending only or primarily to independent variables nonetheless emphasize outcome over process (Locke & Thelen, 1995, p. 344).

In sociology, one of the most prolific comparative methodologists is Charles Ragin. He helpfully showed how different understandings of 'case' affect the conduct and findings of research. Ragin used set theory to develop approaches that drew from both qualitative (case-oriented) and quantitative (variable-oriented) work (1987, 2000, 2008). Ragin argued that quantitative studies tend to distort data, become vague and abstract in a search for maximum generalizability, and overlook important questions. He valued the "conjunctural and complex" vision of causation possible with qualitative comparative analysis (2014). Ragin developed a Boolean logic based on set theory, which used binary scores (0, 1) to code elements of cases and look for set relations (1987). For example, an analyst might consider all the countries that experienced mass protest in the 1980s against the austerity measures imposed by the International Monetary Fund and list causal conditions; the researcher might then consider the negative cases and similarly identify presence or absence of possible causes. The resulting table allows the researcher to consider various combinations of factors and outcomes. Later, Ragin explored the use of "fuzzy sets," which used an ordinal scheme to allow for consideration of phenomena that vary by level or degree. For example, in a study of fragile states (which might, at the risk of oversimplifying, be glossed as a state with weak capacity and legitimacy), 0 might mean "fully out of the set"; lower than 0.5 means "more out than in"; higher than 0.5 but under 1 signals "almost fully in"; and 1.0 means "fully in the set" (2000). Using this approach, Ragin framed cases not as combinations of variables but rather configurations of conditions, thus blurring traditional dichotomies. Nonetheless, Ragin's approach requires the analyst to impose variables on the data and determine the strength of a variable's presence.

From a very different disciplinary perspective, anthropologists generally consider their work to be inherently comparative (e.g., Gingrich & Fox, 2002), even when focused on only one site, given that the ethnographer as the instrument of research is constantly comparing his or her experiences and assumptions to those of study participants.[2] Our CCS approach is heavily influenced by contemporary anthropology, particularly efforts to engage in multi-sited ethnography. This methodology traces people and connections across space and time. As we describe more fully in Chapter 2, multi-sited ethnography does not contrast places assumed to be unrelated; instead, it looks at linkages across place, space, and time. Our heuristic aims to develop an approach to comparison that considers similarities, differences, and possible linkages across sites, across hierarchies of power/levels, and across time.

One effort by educational anthropologist Joseph Tobin and colleagues to develop an unusual approach to comparison merits mention. They used video-cued ethnographic techniques to examine preschool education within the U.S., Japan, and China. In the original study, Tobin et al. (1989) videotaped, in one early childhood location per country, a set of "critical incidents," such as classroom routines, separation, misbehavior, and mixed-aged play. They then presented the video to the educators themselves, to fellow educators in the same location, and to educators of other nationalities in the peer locations; they used the videos as cues to prompt the actors to make sense of and compare actions. As Varenne (2014) suggested, these interviews prompted "meta-cultural" or "meta-ideological" reflections based in a notion of culture as "the deliberate production of something that responds to an uncertainty" (p. 43). In their innovative restudy in the same three countries, Tobin and colleagues (2009) built in two further explicit comparisons. First, based on educator nominations, the researchers selected an additional "innovative" school in each country, prompting comparison with the original school. Second, the researchers returned to the original schools, shooting new videotape of the same category of incidents, thus allowing comparison across time (2009). One limitation is that the studies used nation-state adjectives for cultural practices (e.g., "Japanese culture"); they could be improved by incorporating more clearly a contemporary notion of culture that is not spatially delimited (Steiner-Khamsi, 2014). Nonetheless, these studies provide one methodologically innovative avenue for comparison.

In the multi-disciplinary field of comparative education, as in other fields, comparison has come to mean different things to different people. For many years, there was an underlying assumption that comparison must be cross-national. This trend dates from the 1960s and 1970s, when scholars like Harold Noah and Max Eckstein sought to move the field away from more historically-informed methods and toward a hypothesis-driven social science, as reflected in their book *Toward a Science of Comparative Education* (1969). This tendency persists today in the field of comparative education, if perhaps unconsciously (Phillips & Schweisfurth, 2014). For example, in her review of comparative education publications, Little (2000) pointed out that few articles engage "an explicitly comparative approach" because "the majority of articles focus on single countries" (p. 285). The assumption is that comparison is, by definition, cross-national (or cross-cultural, with culture being used in an erroneous fashion to designate time- and place-bound groups, like a nation-state).

However, contemporary comparative education scholars have vigorously defended the value of other types of comparison. Steiner-Khamsi warned educational policy scholars to avoid methodological nationalism, which is

> the trap of first establishing national boundaries, only to demonstrate afterward that these boundaries have indeed been transcended. [Policy] reforms do not have a home base, a territory, or a nationality and therefore do not 'belong' to a particular educational system.
>
> (2010, p. 327; see also Schriewer, 1990)

Phillips and Schweisfurth also insisted that the state is not sufficiently coherent to serve as an exemplary unit of comparison. They contended that "intranational investigation has been relatively neglected," and "comparativists should seek out units of analysis that are intrinsically appropriate to the task at hand" (2014, p. 115).

Adopting a processual approach, Carney (2009) creatively compared the educational "policyscape" of three countries (Denmark, Nepal, and China) in three different domains (higher education, general education, non-university-based teacher education). According to Carney, a policyscape is an

> educational ideoscape . . . that might capture some essential elements of globalization as a phenomenon (object and process) and provide a tool with which to explore the spread of policy ideas and pedagogical practice across different national school systems.
>
> (2009, p. 68)

Carney demonstrated how a policyscape binds these putatively dissimilar countries together as they reform their education systems in ways that evidence strikingly similar "visions, values, and ideology" (2009, p. 79). He argued that global flows of policies have "dislodged [the state] from its national context and sucked into the disjunctive forces and imaginative regimes of different global 'scapes,' developmental agencies, and their vested interests" while continuing to "mediate the terms on which new regimes and technologies can be received" (2012, p. 4). The notion of policyscapes allows researchers to maintain a certain degree of attention on the state without making it the sole or primary focus of analysis. In such an approach, comparison may be engaged to demonstrate how strikingly dissimilar countries and social or educational challenges might be addressed with similar policies.

Our CCS heuristic draws upon these ideas about and examples of comparison, while taking into account concerns about culture and context, as noted above. We reject the notion of nation-state, place, context, or culture as 'container,' and we eschew the tendency to replace nation-state with a static notion of culture. While we find it useful in research design to consider "units of analysis," we are skeptical about bounding entities, which contravenes our understanding of relevant contexts and processes. Instead, we seek to look at how processes unfold, often influenced by actors and events over time in different locations and at different scales. Such an optic requires a multi-sited, multi-scalar approach. As James Ferguson (2012) explained, using the example of violence in Nigeria's oil-rich delta region, an adequate analysis

> would need to explore local politics, national consciousness, land tenure, histories of ethnic formations, relations between different levels of state bureaucracy, and many other Nigerian realities. But to make sense of these 'local' facts—to bring them into intelligibility—it would also have to explore a range of other questions. What about the East European mafias that illegally buy oil from local strongmen? What about the traffic in arms? How are local struggles for autonomy related to the networks of NGOs and advocacy organizations based in London and elsewhere, which provide both resources and conceptual frames that link local grievances to wider claims? How are the 'social responsibility' policies of big Western oil companies feeding local enmities by dispensing resources to both state governments and ill-defined 'communities'?
>
> (2012, p. 199)

This reflection exemplifies the need for attention to the vertical, horizontal, and especially the transversal, historical elements of the object of study. A fully transversal study of this situation in the Niger Delta would need to address how colonialism shaped the reification of ethnicity, as well as the histories of the oil companies (and potentially their financial and political relationships to the state and local governments) and the relevant NGOs (for examples of such work, see Elyachar, 2005 or Schuller, 2012). Transversal comparison situates all of these elements within a broader historical context, showing how the Delta region was socio-politically produced as a place. In the field of education, a parallel study might engage in a horizontal exploration of local policies that foment ethnic violence in different locations, a vertical examination of national educational bureaucracies, and a transversal investigation of the role of schooling in the evolution of ethnic and racial formations. This optic requires a processual, iterative rethinking of case studies.

In sum, we argue for a view of comparison that is *processual*, in that it considers the cultural production of places and events, as well as the articulation and dearticulation of networks and actors over time and space, rejecting staid notions of culture or context; and one that *constantly compares and contrasts* phenomena and processes in one locale with what has happened in other places and historical moments. Chapter 2 will elaborate the methodological foundation for this heuristic.

Exercise 1.5 Comparison

- What is your notion of comparison? Is it more oriented toward a variance or a processual approach?
- What discipline or field (e.g., political science, anthropology, history, sociology, education, or policy studies) most influences your approach to comparison? How? Why?
- Look at the list of research questions you developed earlier. What sorts of comparisons might you include in the research design for each study?
- Take one of your proposed research questions. Briefly describe how you would build a horizontal, vertical, and transversal comparison into your potential research design.

Chapter Outlines

In this book, we seek to elaborate our conceptual approach to CCS research. In *Chapter 2*, we provide an overview of case study methods. We begin by discussing existing, influential conceptualizations of case studies that are positivist and interpretivist in orientation; we describe the limitations of those approaches. We then explain a process-oriented approach to research and why it is ideal for comparative case studies. In the second section, we explore the methodological influences on the CCS approach, including the extended case method, multi-sited ethnography, and actor network theory. Inspired by and extending those, we provide details about the concepts that undergird our CCS approach, including a critical approach to power relations; a notion of context that is relational and spatial; an emergent and iterative focus on process; a commitment to tracing connections across a spatially dispersed field; the imperative to look at interactionally-produced meanings of events and interactions; and a reconsideration of the possibilities of comparison.

In *Chapter 3* we describe the horizontal axis, which compares how similar policies may unfold in different locations. We first explain the distinction between homologous horizontal comparisons, which use units of analysis with a corresponding position at the same scale (e.g., two schools or two hospitals in one city), and heterologous horizontal comparisons, where the entities are categorically distinct but hold a position more or less at the same scale (such as a school, a clinic, and a community center in one town). We then discuss two methods that are useful in horizontal comparison—interviews and observations. Finally, we offer five examples that illustrate how to use those methods to conduct horizontal comparisons (and, in some instances, how to integrate horizontal with vertical and transversal comparisons).

Chapter 4 describes the vertical axis of comparison, which insists on simultaneous attention to and across multiple scales. Drawing on actor network theory, we conceptualize this interrelation as an assemblage. Assemblages are temporary, shifting alliances or networks of people, objects, and ideas; researchers examine how assemblages are amassed, organized, challenged, and sustained, at least temporarily. The chapter outlines specific methods, including network analysis and critical discourse analysis, to aid in this effort, and it describes at length two studies that illustrate how to conduct a vertical comparison (while embedding horizontal and transversal elements).

Chapter 5 emphasizes the importance of transversal comparison, which historically situates the processes or relations under consideration and traces the creative appropriation of educational policies and practices across time and space. This element is often overlooked by case study research. In this chapter, while reviewing studies that exemplify the transversal axis—including two longitudinal studies of our own—we highlight useful methods, including life histories, oral histories, archival research, and surveys.

Chapter 6 concludes the volume by reiterating the major tenets of comparative case studies. It then reviews a series of questions we are often asked about the CCS approach, including: What is a case? How do I select cases? When is a case not a case? How do I analyze the data? Is the CCS simply too ambitious? Responding to these questions offers a chance to restate and consolidate the main ideas presented across the book, further clarifying the notion of comparative case studies.

Notes

1 Latour explained:

> Macro no longer describes a *wider* or a *larger* site in which the micro would be embedded like some Russian Matryoshka doll, but another equally local, equally micro place, which is *connected* to many others through some medium transporting specific types of traces.
>
> (2005, p. 176)

2 "Cross-cultural" or ethnological studies in anthropology are rare, in part as a response to the controversial mid-twentieth century experiment with the Human Relations Area Files, which collected and contrasted data from across a range of "cultures" using categories that were ethically derived (meaning derived from the perspective of the researcher) and imposed upon the data. Conceptually, cross-cultural comparisons suffer from a series of challenges, including how to demarcate comparable units, the amazing human diversity encompassed by even the simplest of categories, the unfortunate tendency to treat cultural characteristics as stable in order to develop typologies, the fact that cultural studies tend to focus on on-going and incomplete processes, and the way we conceive culture itself (Hirsch et al., 2010). Overall, there is a healthy skepticism in anthropology regarding the tendency of many approaches to reduce complexity in order to facilitate comparisons. We share that concern.

References

Abu-Lughod, J. (1991). Going beyond global babble. In A. D. King (Ed.), *Culture, globalization and the world-system: Contemporary conditions for the representation of identity* (pp. 131–138). Binghamton, NY: State University of New York Press.

Anderson-Levitt, K. M. (2012). Complicating the concept of culture. *Comparative Education* 48(4), 441–454.

Appadurai, A. (1999). Globalization and the research imagination. *International Social Science Journal* 51(160), 229–238.

Ball, S. J. (1994). *Education reform: A critical and post-structural approach*. Buckingham, UK: Open University Press.

Bartlett, L., & Vavrus, F. (2014). Transversing the vertical case study: A methodological approach to studies of educational policy as practice. *Anthropology & Education Quarterly* 45(2), 131–147.

Bennett, A. (2008). Process tracing: A Bayesian perspective. In J. M. Box-Steffensmeier, H. E. Brady & D. Collier (Eds.), *The Oxford handbook of political methodology* (pp. 702–721). Oxford: Oxford University Press.

Bourdieu, P. (1977). *Outline of a theory of practice*. Cambridge, UK: Cambridge University Press.

Bourdieu, P. (1990) *In other words: Essays towards a reflexive sociology* Stanford: Stanford University Press.

Bourdieu, P., & Wacquant, L. J. (1992). *An invitation to reflexive sociology*. Chicago: University of Chicago Press.

Bray, M., & Thomas, R. M. (1995). Levels of comparison in educational studies: Different insights from different literatures and the value of multilevel analyses. *Harvard Educational Review* 65(3), 472–491.

Bronfenbrenner, U. (1977). Toward an experimental ecology of human development. *American Psychologist* 32(7), 513.

Caporaso, J. (2009). Is there a quantitative-qualitative divide in comparative politics? The case of process tracing. In T. Landman & N. Robinson (Eds.), *Sage handbook of comparative politics* (pp. 67–83). Thousand Oaks, CA: Sage.

Carney, S. (2009). Negotiating policy in an age of globalization: Exploring educational "policyscapes" in Denmark, Nepal, and China. *Comparative Education Review* 53(1), 63–88.

Carney, S. (2012). Imagining globalization: Educational policyscapes. In G. Steiner Khamsi & F. Waldow (Eds.), *World yearbook of education 2012* (pp. 339–353). New York: Routledge.

Cole, M. (1996). *Culture in mind*. Cambridge, MA: Harvard University Press.

Cuban, L. (1993). *How teachers taught: Constancy and change in American classrooms, 1890–1990*. New York: Teachers College Press.

de Certeau, M. (1984). *The practice of everyday life*. Berkeley: University of California Press.

Duranti, A., & Goodwin, C. (1992). *Rethinking context: Language as an interactive phenomenon*. London: Cambridge University Press.

Dyson, A. H., & Genishi, C. (2005). *On the case: Approaches to language and literacy research*. New York: Teachers College Press.

Elyachar, J. (2005) *Markets of dispossession: NGOs, economic development and the state in Cairo*. Durham, NC: Duke University Press.

Engeström, Y. (1987). *Learning by expanding: An activity-theoretical approach to developmental research*. Helsinki: Orienta-Konsultit.

Engeström, Y., Miettinen, R., & Punamäki, R. L. (Eds.). (1999). *Perspectives on activity theory*. Cambridge, UK: Cambridge University Press.

Erickson, F. (2011). Culture. In B. A. U. Levinson & M. Pollock (Eds.), *A companion to the anthropology of education* (pp. 25–33). Chichester, UK: Wiley-Blackwell.

Ferguson, J. (2012). Novelty and method: Reflections on global fieldwork. In S. Coleman & P. von Hellermann (Eds.), *Multi-sited ethnography: Problems and possibilities in the translocation of research methods* (pp. 194–208). New York: Routledge.

Fox, R. G., & King, B. J. (Eds.). (2002). *Anthropology beyond culture*. New York: New York University Press.

Garfinkel, H. (1984). *Studies in ethnomethodology*. Cambridge, UK: Polity Press.

Garfinkel, H. (2002). *Ethnomethodology's program: Working out Durkheim's aphorism*. Lanham, MD: Rowman & Littlefield.

Geertz, C. (1973). *The interpretation of cultures*. New York: Basic Books.

Geertz, C. (1996). Afterword. In S. Feld & K. H. Basso (Eds.), *Senses of place* (pp. 259–262). Santa Fe, NM: School of American Research Press.

George, A. L., & Bennett, A. (2004). *Case studies and theory development in the social sciences*. Cambridge, MA: MIT Press.

Gerring, J. (2004). What is a case study and what is it good for? *American Political Science Review* 98(2), 341–354.

Giddens, A. (1984). *The constitution of society: Outline of the theory of structuration*. Berkeley: University of California Press.

Gingrich, A., & Fox, R. G. (Eds.). (2002). *Anthropology by comparison*. New York: Routledge.

Gisselquist, R. M. (2014). Paired comparison and theory development: Considerations for case selection. *PS: Political Science & Politics* 47(2), 477–484.

Goldman, M. (2006). *Imperial nature: The World Bank and struggles for social justice in the age of globalization*. New Haven, CT: Yale University Press.

Gupta, A., & Ferguson, J. (1992). Beyond 'culture': Space, identity, and the politics of difference. *Cultural Anthropology* 7, 6–23.

Gupta, A., & Ferguson, J. (1997). Culture, power, place: Ethnography at the end of an era. In A. Gupta & J. Ferguson (Eds.), *Culture, power, place: Explorations in critical anthropology* (pp. 1–32). Durham, NC: Duke University Press.

Hamann, E. T., & Rosen, L. (2011). What makes the anthropology of educational policy implementation 'anthropological'? In B. A. U. Levinson & M. Pollock (Eds.), *A companion to the anthropology of education* (pp. 461–477). Chichester, UK: Wiley-Blackwell.

Hannerz, U. (2006). Studying down, up, sideways, through, backwards, forwards, away and at home: Reflections on the field worries of an expansive discipline. In S. M. Coleman & P. Collins (Eds.), *Locating the field: Space, place and context in anthropology* (pp. 23–41). Oxford, UK: Berg.

Hirsch, J., Wardlow, H., Smith, D. J., Phinney, H., Parikh, S., & Nathanson, C. (2010). *The secret: Love, marriage and HIV*. Nashville, TN: Vanderbilt University Press.

Ho, K. (2009). *Liquidated: An ethnography of Wall Street*. Durham, NC: Duke University Press.

Landman, T., & Robinson, N. (Eds.). (2009). *Sage handbook of comparative politics*. Thousand Oaks, CA: Sage.

Larsen, M. A., & Beech, J. (2014). Spatial theorizing in comparative and international education research. *Comparative Education Review* 58(2), 191–214.

Latour, B. (2005). *Reassembling the social: An introduction to actor-network theory*. Oxford: Oxford University Press.

Leander, K. (2002). *Situated literacies, digital practices, and the constitution of space-time*. Paper presented at the National Reading Conference, Miami, FL.

Leander, K., & Sheehy, M. (Eds.). (2004). *Spatializing literacy research and practice*. New York: Peter Lang.

Levinson, B. A. U., & Sutton, M. (2001). Policy as/in practice: Developing a sociocultural approach to the study of educational policy. In M. Sutton & B. A. U. Levinson (Eds.),

Policy as practice: Toward a comparative sociocultural analysis of educational policy (pp. 1–22). Westport, CT: Ablex.

Levinson, B. A. U., Sutton, M., & Winstead, T. (2009). Education policy as a practice of power: Theoretical tools, ethnographic methods, democratic options. *Educational Policy 23*(6), 767–795.

Little, A. (2000). Development studies and comparative education: Context, content, comparison and contributors. *Comparative Education 36*(3), 279–296.

Locke, R. M., & Thelen, K. (1995). Apples and oranges revisited: Contextualized comparisons and the study of comparative labor politics. *Politics and Society 23*, 337–368.

Massey, D. (1991). A global sense of place. *Marxism Today 38*, 24–29.

Massey, D. (2005). *For space*. London: Sage.

Maxwell, J. (2013). *Qualitative research design: An interactive approach*. Thousand Oaks, CA: Sage.

McDermott, R., & Varenne, H. (1995). Culture as disability. *Anthropology & Education Quarterly 26*(3), 324–348.

Menken, K., & García, O. (Eds.). (2010). *Negotiating language education policies: Educators as policymakers*. New York: Routledge.

Middleton, S. (2014). *Henri Lefebvre and education: Space, history, theory*. New York: Routledge.

Nadai, E., & Maeder, C. (2005). Fuzzy fields: Multi-sited ethnography in sociological research. *Forum Qualitative Sozialforschung / Forum: Qualitative Social Research*, 6(3), Art. 28. Available at http://www.qualitative-research.net/index.php/fqs/article/view/22/47 on 25 April 2016.

Nespor, J. (1997). *Tangled up in school*. Mahwah, NJ: Lawrence Erlbaum Associates.

Nespor, J. (2004). Educational scale-making. *Pedagogy, Culture & Society 12*(3), 309–326.

Noah, H. J., & Eckstein, M. A. (1969). *Toward a science of comparative education*. London: MacMillan Company.

Oke, N. (2009). Globalizing time and space: Temporal and spatial considerations in discourses of globalization. *International Political Sociology 3*(3), 310–326.

Ortner, S. B. (1984). Theory in anthropology since the sixties. *Comparative Studies in Society and History 26*(1), 126–166.

Ortner, S. B. (Ed.). (1999). *The fate of 'culture': Geertz and beyond*. Cambridge: Harvard University Press.

Phillips, D., & Schweisfurth, M. (2014). *Comparative and international education: An introduction to theory, method, and practice*. New York: Bloomsbury.

Ragin, C. C. (1987). *The comparative method: Moving beyond qualitative and quantitative methods*. Berkeley: University of California.

Ragin, C. C. (2000). *Fuzzy set social science*. Chicago: University of Chicago Press.

Ragin, C. C. (2008). *Redesigning social inquiry: Set relations in social research*. Chicago: University of Chicago Press.

Ragin, C. C. (2014). *The comparative method: Moving beyond qualitative and quantitative strategies*. Berkeley: University of California Press.

Ravitch, D. (1983). *The troubled crusade: American education, 1945–1980*. New York: Basic Books.

Robertson, S. (2012). Researching global education policy: Angles in/on/out. In A. Verger, M. Novelli, & H. K. Altinyelken (Eds.), *Global education policy and international development: New agendas, issues and practices* (pp. 33–52). New York: Continuum.

Roseberry, W. (1989). *Anthropologies and histories: Essays in culture, history, and political economy.* New Brunswick, NJ: Rutgers University Press.

Schriewer, J. (1990). The method of comparison and the need for externalization: Methodological criteria and sociological concepts. In J. Schriewer, in cooperation with B. Holmes (Eds.), *Theories and methods in comparative education* (pp. 25–83). Frankfurt: Peter Lang.

Schuller, M. (2012). *Killing with kindness: Haiti, international aid, and NGOs.* New Brunswick, NJ: Rutgers University Press.

Schweisfurth, M. (2013). *Learner-centred education in international perspective: Whose pedagogy for whose development?* New York: Routledge.

Scola, N. (2012, April 14). Exposing ALEC: How conservative-backed state laws are all connected. *The Atlantic.* Available at http://www.theatlantic.com/politics/archive/2012/04/exposing-alec-how-conservative-backed-state-laws-are-all-connected/255869/.

Shore, C., & Wright, S. (1997). *Anthropology of policy: Critical perspectives on governance and power.* London: Routledge.

Simmons, E. S., & Smith, N. R. (2015). The case for comparative ethnography. *Qualitative and Multi-Method Research 13*(2), 13–18.

Slater, D., & Ziblatt, D. (2013). The enduring indispensability of the controlled comparison. *Comparative Political Studies 46*(10), 1301–1327.

Snyder, R. (2001). Scaling down: The subnational comparative method. *Studies in Comparative International Development 36*(1), 93–110.

Steiner-Khamsi, G. (2010). The politics and economics of comparison. *Comparative Education Review 54*(3), 323–342.

Steiner-Khamsi, G. (2014). Comparison and context: The interdisciplinary approach to the comparative study of education. *Current Issues in Comparative Education 16*, 2. Available at http://www.tc.columbia.edu/cice/pdf/33066_16_2_Gita_Steiner-Khamsi.pdf.

Street, B. (1993). Culture is a verb: Anthropological aspects of language and cultural process. In D. Graddol, L. Thompson & M. Byram (Eds.), *Language and culture* (pp. 23–43). Clevedon, UK: British Association for Applied Linguistics.

Tarrow, S. (2010). The strategy of paired comparison: Toward a theory of practice. *Comparative Political Studies 43*(2), 230–259.

Taylor, C., Rees, G., Sloan, L., & Davies, R. (2013). Creating an inclusive higher education system? Progression and outcomes of students from low participation neighbourhoods at a Welsh university. *Contemporary Wales 26*(1), 138–161.

Tobin, J., Wu, D. Y. H., & Davidson, D. H. (1989). *Preschool in three cultures: Japan, China, and the United States.* New Haven, CT: Yale University Press.

Tobin, J., Hsueh, Y., & Karasawa, M. (2009). *Preschool in three cultures revisited: China, Japan, and the United States.* Chicago: University of Chicago Press.

Tsing, A. L. (2005). *Friction: An ethnography of global connections.* Princeton: Princeton University Press.

Varenne, H. (2014). Comments on Tobin's contribution to comparative research in anthropology and in education. *Current Issues in Comparative Education 16*(2), 44–48.

Vavrus, F. (2015). Topographies of power: A critical historical geography of schooling in Tanzania. *Comparative Education 1*–21. DOI: 10.1080/03050068.2015.1112567.

Vavrus, F., & Bartlett, L. (2006). Comparatively knowing: Making a case for the vertical case study. *Current Issues in Comparative Education 8*(2), 95–103.

Vavrus, F., & Bartlett, L. (2009). *Critical approaches to comparative education: Vertical case studies from Africa, Europe, the Middle East, and the Americas*. New York: Palgrave Macmillan.

Vavrus, F., & Bartlett, L. (2012). Comparative pedagogies and epistemological diversity: Social and material contexts of teaching in Tanzania. *Comparative Education Review* 56(4), 634–658.

Vavrus, F., & Bartlett, L. (2013). *Teaching in tension: International pedagogies, national policies, and teachers' practices in Tanzania*. Rotterdam: Sense Publishers.

Webb, T., & Mkongo, S. (2013). Classroom discourse. In F. Vavrus & L. Bartlett (Eds.), *Teaching in tension: International pedagogies, "national policies, and teachers" practices in Tanzania* (pp. 149–168). Rotterdam: Sense Publishers.

2 Case Studies

An Overview

Case study methodology is widely used across multiple disciplines and fields. But what is a case, and what is a case study? Think of your own understanding of a case study. How might you define it? In his introduction to the fascinating edited volume called *What Is a Case?*, Charles Ragin argued that scholars use the word case "with relatively little consideration of the theories and metatheories embedded in these terms or in the methods that use cases" (1992, p. 1). Case is often defined as place. Researchers may use 'case' to mean one setting, place, or institution, or they may use 'case' for both the institution (or place or setting) *and* each person in it. We may also use case interchangeably with 'units of analysis,' but this can be problematic because it does not sufficiently separate the categories we use to organize our data and the categories we construct based on our theoretical framework. We may assume, said Ragin, that cases are both "similar enough and separate enough to permit treating them as comparable instances of the same general phenomenon" (p. 1). In his essay, Ragin posed a series of provocative questions: What is the relationship between a case and a variable? Are there times when these mean the same thing? What is the difference between case-driven studies and variable-driven case studies? Is a case study constituted by empirical units (e.g., a state, or a hospital) or theoretical constructs? Finally, are cases discovered or developed over the course of conducting research, or are they "general and relatively external to conduct of research" (p. 8)? The answer to each of these questions has implications for how a researcher thinks about and uses case studies.

In conceptualizing case studies, we begin from the premise that the definition of case study research depends on the epistemology and methodology engaged by the author. Thus, we believe it is important to discuss the distinction between variance-oriented, interpretivist, and process-oriented approaches case study research and why this is a useful way of categorizing the relevant literature (Maxwell, 2013). In this chapter, we go into greater detail in explaining why we favor the latter—process-oriented approaches— and how they are more appropriate for a comparative case study (CCS). We begin in the first section by discussing traditional conceptualizations of case studies that are more variance-focused or more interpretivist in orientation. We pinpoint the limitations of traditional models of case studies, focusing on the frequently narrow notions of culture, context, and comparison that we introduced in the last chapter, and we explain the value of a process-oriented approach. We follow this discussion in the second section that explores the methodological foundations of the CCS approach as a means of differentiating it from these other orientations. Specifically, we describe the influence on our approach of the extended case method, multi-sited and multi-scalar ethnography, and actor network theory. These bodies of work inform the approach that we develop in this book. The third section provides details about the key ideas that undergird our CCS approach. These notions include a critical approach to power relations; reconceptualizing space, scale, and context; focusing on the processes through which events unfold, which implies a distinct, critical approach to thinking about causality; and understanding the imperative to look at interactionally-produced meanings of events and interactions.

Traditional Case Study Approaches

Existing, influential conceptualizations of case studies can be usefully divided into three categories: variance-oriented, interpretivist, and process-oriented. In this section, we consider each of these approaches, and we also outline some of the limitations of existing, prominent approaches.

Variance-Oriented Case Studies

As we discussed in the previous chapter, what Maxwell called "variance-oriented" approaches dominate in case study work in many disciplines—particularly political science and sociology. Variance-oriented work

> deals with variables and the correlations among them; it is based on an analysis of the contributions of differences in values of particular variables to differences in other variables. The comparison of conditions or groups in which the presumed causal factor takes different values, while other factors are held constant or statistically controlled, is central to this approach to causation . . . . Thus, variance theory tends to be associated with research that employs experimental or correlational designs, quantitative measurement, and statistical analysis.
>
> (Maxwell, 2004, pp. 4–5)[1]

These approaches to case study research embrace neo-positivism as an epistemological stance for case study research. At the risk of oversimplifying, we can say that neo-positivism adopts the view that the world operates by laws of cause and effect and that these laws can be discovered through scientific methods like observation. These entail a process of posing a question (often about causal relations), developing hypotheses, identifying variables, developing and operationalizing constructs that can be observed and measured, and analyzing the results (often using statistical means) (Trochim, 2006).

Popular texts on research methodologies that are not affiliated with a specific discipline often adopt some of the elements of variance approaches, though they are considerably chastened in their aspirations. Such efforts are represented by the influential work of Robert Yin, a social scientist with a background in quantitative and experimental methods. Yin's book, *Case Study Research* (in its fifth edition at the time of our writing), has shaped research methods for decades. Yin (2014) offered the following definition of a case study:

> A case study is an empirical inquiry that investigates a contemporary phenomenon (the case) in-depth and within its real-world context, especially when the boundaries between phenomenon and context may not be clearly evident. In other words, you would want to do case study research because you want to understand a real world case and assume that such an understanding is likely to involve important contextual conditions pertinent to your case.
>
> (p. 16)

Yin's work, developed over a long period of time, is instructive and insightful. It merits careful review. However, here we wish to highlight a few features of Yin's definition that we find problematic.

First, for Yin, case study methods focus on "contemporary phenomena." While he acknowledged that this "does not exclude the recent past," he warned the reader to avoid "events extending back to the 'dead' past, where no direct observations can be made and no people are alive to be interviewed" (p. 24). This limited notion of the value or import of history stands in direct contrast to the transversal element of the CCS approach.

Second, Yin's comment about the blurred boundaries between phenomenon and context suggests his struggle over conceptualizing context and its relation to delineating a "case." For Yin, case study was distinguished from experiments, which "separate a phenomenon from its context," and surveys, whose "ability to investigate the context is extremely limited" (p. 17). In this and other quotes, Yin seemed to define case as place and conflate case and context, stating that "the boundaries between phenomenon and context may not be clearly evident" (2014, p. 16). While we share his positive valuation of naturalistic inquiry, we are concerned at this notion of context, which lends itself to several problems. One is that it runs the risk of promoting a "context as container" notion, where the immediate temporal and geographic/place-based elements of the study are the only ones seen as relevant. As Ragin (1992) suggested, it demonstrates a fuzzy conflation of the place and the phenomenon, obfuscating the "theories and metatheories embedded in these terms" (p. 1). Another is that it limits the aspiration to generate theory or insights that will generalize to other cases.

Third, grappling with his variance logic, Yin assumed that we can create a complex case study through the amalgamation of variables. He contended that case studies will have "many more variables of interest than data points," and he suggested that one can address this issue by using multiple methods of data collection that can be triangulated as a means of verifying the truthfulness of the data (2014, pp. 16–17). Though he tried to soften a variable-based logic, Yin remained beholden to it, as when he wrote:

> Having *more variables of interest than data points* arises from the complexity of the case and its context (hence, many variables), with the case being the only 'data point.' The use of this language does not mean that case studies are variable-based; on the contrary, the multiplicity of variables raises doubts about the usefulness of conventional variable-based methods in analyzing case study data, hence favoring holistic approaches.
>
> (2011, p. 24)

What does it mean to suggest that the case is the only "data point"? We contend that a case is not a single 'data point'; surely, any good case study will present a multitude of data about some phenomenon of interest. Why did Yin speak the language of variables, as if the case study were a weak version of inquiry, even as he questioned the "usefulness of conventional variable-based methods"? What did Yin mean by "holistic approaches"? Elsewhere, Yin stated that the "case study method allows investigators to retain the holistic and meaningful characteristics of real-life events" (2009, p. 4). Here, we understand that he was trying to signal the irreducibility of context. However, such a stance led Yin to a sense that "context" must be taken as a whole. Holism makes analysis difficult and leads the researcher toward mere description.

Fourth, for Yin, an essential step of defining the study is "bounding the case." He wrote:

> Once the general definition of the case has been established, other clarifications – sometimes called bounding the case – become important. If the unit of analysis is a small group, for instance, the persons to be included within the group must be distinguished from those who were outside of it …. Similarly if the case is about the local services and a specific geographic area, you need to decide which services to cover …. [Clarify the boundaries of your case] with regard to the time covered by the case study; the relevant social group, organization, or geographic area; the type of evidence to be collected; and the priorities for data collection and analysis.
>
> (2011, pp. 33–34)

To be fair, Yin did acknowledge that the research design might change over time;[2] however, his emphasis on bounding is marked. Yin is not alone in his concern with "bounding" the case. Case study methodologists Creswell (2013) and Stake (1995) also suggested bounding by time and activity, and Miles and Huberman (1994) recommended bounding by definition and context. Each insists that bounding the case maintains a reasonable and feasible scope for the study. We find this notion of bounding the case from the outset to be problematic. It aligns more fully with a neo-positivist and variance-oriented design, which predefines variables and hypothesizes relationships, than it does with the iterative, processual designs more common in qualitative work. As we will explain further below, *a priori* efforts to "bound the case" rely on limited notions of context and comparison.

Fifth, the overall tone of Yin's work emphasizes variance and a neo-positivist epistemology. Yin applied positivist notions of validity to case study work. He urged readers to attend to construct validity, or the appropriateness of inferences made on the basis of observations or measurements, which for Yin is achieved through multiple sources of evidence, by establishing a chain of evidence, and by having key informants review reports. He also called on researchers to focus on internal validity, achieved through pattern matching, explanation building, and logical models. In addition, he emphasized external validity (generalizability). Like many others, Yin promoted a distinct notion of generalizability for single case studies. He averred that "case studies, like experiments, are generalizable to theoretical propositions and not to populations or universes" (2011, p. 21). Generalization, he said, can be a lesson learned or hypothesis applicable to other situations (2011). Yin warned against efforts to use single case studies for statistical generalization, as is common in quantitative studies (2011). For multiple case studies, Yin urged replication to achieve external validity. Indeed, Yin considered replication to be the primary value of designs that include multiple case studies. He encouraged readers to "consider multiple cases as one would consider multiple experiments—that is, to follow a 'replication' design" by selecting cases that are expected to either produce similar results or produce different results for a predictable reason (2014, p. 57). Yin praised a tight, structured design for case studies and, in so doing, promoted concepts and approaches that are more appropriate for variance-oriented studies than the processual approach we advocate for in this book.

Sixth, Yin's work understates the value of case studies in social science research. For example, Yin (2009) declared three types of case studies: exploratory (collecting data and looking for patterns), descriptive (considering possible theories to frame the study and questions), and explanatory (explaining the how or why of the topic or population studied). Of these, we feel only an explanatory case rises to the level of significance expected of most social science research. Cases that are merely descriptive or exploratory are rarely given much credence. Thus, Yin's view that case study research is often exploratory or descriptive denigrates it as an approach to meaningful scholarship. It is on this point that we firmly disagree.

Yin's variance-oriented approach to case study research has had a far-ranging impact on research in numerous fields, including the fields of education and policy studies in which we primarily work. However, we have noted some of its shortcomings and where we diverge from him. In sum, we find great utility in maintaining a historical perspective on comparative research. Even if the historical (transversal) comparison is not the central focus of a CCS, it can provide essential background information for the study. We also employ a different notion of context which, we argue, allows us to sidestep the conflation of case and context. Further, our notion of context as historically produced and multi-scalar redirects the impetus to treat a case as "holistic" and hence as difficult to analyze. In addition, we question the need to "bound" the case, *a priori*, in any definitive sense; instead, we promote careful, evolving, iterative attention to the contours of the research design and how boundaries perceived by participants come to be meaningful. We also differ from Yin in his reliance on the concepts of validity, reliability, and generalizability, as these are not necessarily the most appropriate ways to apprehend the quality of a process-oriented study. Some scholars recommend a parallel framework of trustworthiness, with a focus on the adequacy of the data and the interpretation, as more congruent with naturalistic research (Guba & Lincoln, 1994; Lincoln & Guba, 1985, 1986). Many have questioned the appropriateness of reliability as a standard for any qualitative work, and most would agree that qualitative researchers generalize through theory, not statistically (e.g., Willis & Trondman, 2000; Wherry, 2015; Gomm, Hammersley, & Foster, 2000). Finally, Yin seems to lack a clear understanding of how to engage comparison other than by embracing a logic of replication, which runs counter to a process-oriented approach to comparison as we advocate.

Exercise 2.1 Variance-Oriented Case Studies

Go back to your review of the case study literature in your field that you began in Chapter 1. Identify a variance-oriented case study.

- How does the case deal with the notions of context, culture, and comparison, if at all? How does it deal with variance or variables? How does it discuss questions of research quality—does it engage the concepts of validity, reliability, or generalizability? What are its overall strengths? What are its weaknesses?

Think of the topic and research questions you identified for your study in Chapter 1.

- How could you revise the questions to make them more appropriate for a variance-oriented approach to case studies? In what ways would this strengthen your original questions? In what ways would it weaken the questions?

Interpretivist Case Studies

Diverging from the variance-oriented tradition, interpretivist case studies attempt to understand participants' sense-making of events or phenomena.

Rooted in a social constructivist notion of reality, they emphasize symbolic aspects of experience, asking how and why people act in certain ways, and exploring the meanings they generate.

Interpretivist approaches to case studies are arguably best exemplified by the influential work of Robert Stake, whose aptly titled 1995 methods book was called *The Art of Case Study Research*. Influenced by his background in psychometrics and educational assessment, but also by his reading of biography and ethnography, he compared case study work to creating art (1995). Stake addressed a range of interpretive orientations toward case study research, including "naturalistic, holistic, ethnographic, phenomenological, and biographic research methods" (1995, p. xi). Stake posited that "most contemporary qualitative researchers hold that knowledge is constructed rather than discovered" (1995, p. 99). He emphasized a focus on meaning, stating that "the ethnographic ethos of *interpretive* study, seeking out emic meanings held by the people within the case, is strong" (1995, p. 240). He celebrated the particular and the unique, and, in comparison to Yin and his quite structured case study approach, Stake promoted a flexible design that shifts in the course of research. He wrote:

> We cannot know at the outset what the issues, the perceptions, the theory will be. Case researchers enter the scene expecting, even knowing, that certain events, problems, relationships will be important, yet discover that some actually are of little consequence.
>
> (1994, pp. 240–241)

For Stake, cases might be valued for their "intrinsic" value to better understand a specific case, or they may be "instrumental" if they serve to provide theoretical insights or reconsider generalizations (2003, pp. 136–138). In these ways, Stake's representation of case study methods is heavily interpretivist in orientation, and we would agree with much of this.

However, there are important ways in which we diverge from Stake's interpretivist orientation. First, while we acknowledge that any study of humans should consider the cultural production of meanings and how they influence actions, we would not wish to ignore power relations or social structures, which are underemphasized in Stake's presentation of case studies.

Second, Stake affirmed "understanding of the case rather than generalization beyond" (1994, p. 236), and he suggested that "the end result regularly presents something unique" (1994, p. 238). While we might not embrace a neo-positivist notion of generalization, we would certainly not wish to forsake the power of cases to generate theoretical insights that transfer to other cases. Indeed, the question of generalizability is one of the main misunderstandings of case studies identified by Flyvbjerg (2011), who asserted that "the case study is ideal for generalizing using the type of test that Karl Popper called 'falsification,'" wherein "if just one observation does not fit with the proposition, it is considered not valid generally and must therefore be either revised or rejected" (2011, p. 305). We would argue that, beyond falsification, cases generate rich theoretical insights that transfer to other times and places.

Third, Stake claimed that researchers using qualitative methods can create a case that can "tell its own story" (p. 239). While we favor rich, detailed narratives, we believe that this stance ignores the power dynamics inherent in social research whereby the researcher is typically the one who makes data selection decisions about what will go into the case study. It also does not take into account the politics of representation—meaning who gets to represent whom and how in a research project, and it does not sufficiently consider the need for ethical engagement and reflexivity on the part of the researcher throughout the research process.

Fourth, Stake adopted a functionalist notion of cases that relies on the sense of a case as a "system." He wrote that the case is a "bounded system" with

> working parts; it is purposive; it often has a self. It is an integrated system .... Its behavior is patterned. Coherence and sequence are prominent. It is common to recognize that certain features are within the system, within the boundaries of the case, and other features outside ... are significant as context.
>
> (2003, p. 135; 1994, p. 237)

By insisting on a notion of the case as "bounded" and "coherent," Stake's approach has the same shortcomings regarding context and comparison as Yin. We contend that boundaries are not found; they are made by social actors, including by researchers, whose demarcations can often seem quite arbitrary and can have the effect of sealing off the case hermetically from other places, times, and influences.

Fifth, in his early work, Stake (like Yin) was circumspect about the value of comparison. He acknowledged the value of what he called a collective case study, in which an instrumental case (selected for the insight it can provide to an issue or theory) is "extended to several cases" that "may be similar or dissimilar," in an effort to generate more informed theory about the wider array of cases (2003, pp. 137–138). However, valuing the particular elements of each case, Stake warned that "direct comparison diminishes the opportunity to learn from" the case (1994, p. 240). He continued: "I see comparison as an epistemological function competing with learning about and from the particular case. Comparison is a powerful conceptual mechanism, fixing attention upon the few attributes being compared and obscuring other knowledge about the case" (1994, p. 242). In such moments, Stake is reacting to a variable-based notion of comparison, in which variables are isolated from each other and from context or processes. He contrasted comparison to thick description, and he stated that comparison downplays "uniqueness and complexities" (2003, pp. 148–149).

In a later publication, Stake took a more sanguine view of comparison, acknowledging the value of the multiple case study. He described the multiple case study as

> a special effort to examine something having lots of cases, parts, or members …. We seek to understand better how this whole … [or] 'quintain,' operates in different situations. The unique life of the case is interesting for what it can reveal about the quintain.
>
> (2006, p. vi)

The quintain, then, is what is being sought across cases. Unfortunately, the concept as presented by Stake remains rather confusing. At some moments, Stake referred to the quintain as a whole that is greater than the sum of its parts. It appears to be an ideal type that is reached inductively through review of cases. Yet, in his book, the quintain also appears to be something like the least common denominator, or the themes that are adequately present across the cases. In Stake's 2006 book, the quintain was the Step by Step program, a child-centered and inclusive early childhood program funded throughout the global South by the Open Society Foundations. To determine which cases to include, Stake announced three main criteria: "Is the case relevant to the quintain? Do the cases provide diversity across contexts? Do the cases provide good opportunities to learn about complexity and contexts?" (p. 23). It is not entirely clear here what he means by context. He also acknowledged that access and feasibility shape case selection. To analyze comparative cases, Stake recommended looking for "correspondence," which he also called covariation and correlation. Correspondence reveals "some of the 'interactivity' of the case—that is, some ways in which the activity of the case interacts with its contexts" (Stake, 2006, p. 28). Thus, for Stake, the comparison of multiple case studies illuminates some larger phenomenon as well as how context shapes social life.

Our CCS heuristic would agree with Stake about the value of multiple cases. While the notion of 'quintain' is a bit obscure, we would happily substitute 'phenomenon,' or possibly stretch the idea to include 'policy.' However, we encourage comparison across three axes: a horizontal look that not only *contrasts* one case (e.g., one country's program) with another, but also traces social actors, documents, or other influences *across* these cases; a vertical comparison of influences at different levels (e.g., from the donor, the Open Society Foundations, to national policy actors, or from national to local policy actors); and a transversal comparison to previous early childhood programs, which would entail attending to how the notion of childhood itself evolved over time in that political, economic, social, and cultural context.

Perhaps as influential as Yin and Stake's methods publications, at least in some fields, is Sharan Merriam's work on case studies, which is also strongly rooted in an interpretivist stance. She stated that "the key philosophical assumption upon which all types of qualitative research are based is the view that reality is constructed by individuals interacting with their social worlds" (1998, p. 6). Further, she averred "that reality is not an objective entity; rather, there are multiple interpretations of reality" (1998, p. 22). Therefore, espousing this philosophical assumption, the primary interest of qualitative researchers is to understand the meaning or knowledge constructed by people. In other words, what really intrigues qualitative researchers is the way people make sense of their experiences. As an interpretivist, Merriam (1998) emphasized that researchers should use inductive reasoning to derive analytical statements.

Like Yin and Stake, Merriam (1998) was concerned with bounding the case. She wrote:

> The single most defining characteristic of case study research lies in delimiting the object of study, the case. Smith's (1978) notion of the case as a *bounded system* comes closest to my understanding of what defines this type of research …. [T]he case is a thing, a single entity, a unit around which there are boundaries …. If the phenomenon you are interested in studying is not intrinsically bounded, it is not a case.
>
> (1998, p. 27)

Merriam's view appears to be shaped by Miles and Huberman's (1994) understanding of "the case as a phenomenon of some sort occurring in a bounded context" (cited in Merriam, 1998, p. 27). This focus on bounding is distinct from our spatially and relationally informed understanding of context and our processual notion of culture.

This sense of context also seems to be in tension with Merriam's focus on process. Like Yin (1994), who argued that case studies are best for addressing how and why questions, Merriam contended, "Case study is a particularly suitable design if you are interested in process" (1998, p. 33). She defined process to include causal explanations of impact or outcomes. However, her discussion of process is quite limited; it does not address the dynamic historical and cultural production of meanings and structures that is central to the CCS approach.

Furthermore, in our opinion, Merriam retained a reduced notion of the theoretical possibilities of case studies, as did Yin and Stake. She defined three types of cases (particularistic, descriptive, and heuristic, meant to increase understanding of the case and discovery of new meaning) and three purposes for them (descriptive, interpretive, and evaluative) (1998, p. 30). These descriptions remain limited to the particularistic and descriptive, declaring a reduced aspiration for greater theoretical import.

The move away from a tightly prescriptive variance-oriented view of case study research as one finds in Yin's work to Merriam and Stake's more interpretivist approach is important to note, but the work of these scholars also suffers from a tendency to refer to a vague sense of *holism*. Stake described four defining characteristics of qualitative case studies: they are holistic, empirical, interpretive, and empathic (focused on meaning). For Stake, holistic referred to the interrelationship between phenomenon (case) and context. Merriam similarly described a qualitative case study as "an intensive, holistic description and analysis of a bounded phenomenon ..." (p. xiii). She later stated, "One of the assumptions underlying qualitative research is that reality is holistic, multidimensional, and ever-changing; it is not a single, fixed, objective phenomenon waiting to be discovered, observed, and measured as in quantitative research" (1998, p. 202). Even Yin (2014) distinguished case studies by contrasting those that are "holistic" (requiring one unit of analysis) to those that are "embedded" (requiring multiple units of analysis).

We find this repeated reference to holism troubling. Holism is a concept linked to a traditional notion of culture and a functionalist theoretical stance. Classical ethnographies aimed to portray a whole way of life, which "implied a coherence of discrete cultures, a timeless 'ethnographic present'" (O'Reilly, 2009, p. 100). In its contemporary form, holism denotes a respect for context (and contextual validity). However, the claim to value holism is an effort to distinguish, but ultimately conflates, case and context (often defined as place), and it is premised upon a bounded view of culture. It also defines out of the realm of study far-flung factors and processes that may be immensely relevant for understanding how *a sense of boundedness* is socially and historically produced. The notion of holism used in interpretive case studies is limited to thick description, to a dedication to "the particular," and to a reduced notion of context that does not attend to how processes, politics, and ideoscapes— the ideologies and other political images that circulate globally (Appadurai, 1996)—at other scales impinge upon the case. Holism is surprisingly limited and rather blind to historical, social, and economic trends. Instead of this *a priori* bounding of the case to the 'particular,' we propose an iterative and contingent tracing of relevant factors, actors, and features.

Exercise 2.2 Interpretivist Case Studies

Go back to your review of the literature in your relevant fields. Identify an interpretivist case study based on the description of their common features discussed above.

- How does the case deal with the notions of context, culture, and comparison, if at all? How does it deal with meaning as generated by participants? How does it address questions of research quality, generalizability, and significance? What are its strengths? What are its weaknesses?

Think of the topic and research questions you identified for your study in Chapter 1.

- How could you revise the questions to make them more appropriate for an interpretivist case studies? In what ways would this strengthen your original questions? In what ways would it weaken the questions?

Process-Oriented Approaches and the CCS Approach

As we have already hinted, the CCS approach diverges from established approaches in several important ways. To begin, it adopts what Maxwell called a *process orientation*. Process approaches "tend to see the world in terms of people, situations, events, and the processes that connect these; explanation is based on an analysis of how some situations and events influence others" (2013, p. 29). Notably, this approach eschews the interpretive refusal to consider causation, but it also avoids the variance-oriented notion of causation. As Maxwell explained:

> Quantitative researchers tend to be interested in whether and to what extent variance in x causes variance in y. Qualitative researchers, on the other hand, tend to ask *how* x plays a role in causing y, what the *process* is that connects x and y.
>
> (2013, p. 31)

Thus, the process-oriented comparison inherent to our notion of comparative case studies insists on an *emergent design*, one hallmark of qualitative research. As Becker (2009) wrote, qualitative researchers

> don't fully specify methods, theory, or data when they begin their research. They start out with ideas, orienting perspectives, or even specific hypotheses, but once they begin, they investigate new leads; apply useful theoretical ideas to the (sometimes unexpected) evidence they gather; and, in other ways, conduct a systematic and rigorous scientific investigation. Each interview and each day's observations produce ideas tested against relevant data. Not fully pre-specifying these ideas and procedures, as well as being ready to change them when their findings require it, are not flaws, but rather two of the great strengths of qualitative research, making possible efficient development and testing of hypotheses.
>
> (p. 548)

Because qualitative studies are emergent, researchers have to make explicit what Heath and Street (2008, p. 56) called "decision rules," or decisions about how to focus or expand the study. These should be noted in one's fieldnotes, and could be reproduced as a sort of "audit trail" (e.g., Lincoln & Guba, 1985). The need for an emergent design is in conflict with the constant admonition in the traditional case study literature to "bound" the case. With this more process-oriented understanding in mind, we should be aware that some studies may be more pre-structured than others; the degree of flexibility will depend on the study's aims, the researcher's motivations, skills, and interests, and the available time and resources, among other things.

The CCS approach does not start with a bounded case. The effort to "bound" a case relies on a problematic notion of culture, place, and community; it also, quite inappropriately, defines out of the realm of study factors that may well be very relevant, such as historical circumstances that date back decades or more. Comparative case studies resist the holism of many traditional case studies, which stubbornly refuse to distinguish phenomenon from context, often defined implicitly as place. It is essential to divorce the phenomenon of interest from the context in order to gain analytical purchase. As Geertz (1973, p. 22) famously explained, "The locus of the study is not the object of study." At the same time, even while including multiple sites and cases, a comparative case study seeks not to flatten the cases by ignoring valuable contextual information or imposing concepts or categories taken from one site onto another (van der Veer, 2016). They seek to disrupt dichotomies, static categories, and taken-for-granted notions of what is going on (Heath & Street, 2008).

Instead of this *a priori* bounding of the case, the CCS approach features an iterative and contingent tracing of relevant factors, actors, and features. The approach is aimed at exploring the historical and contemporary processes that have produced *a sense of* shared place, purpose, or identity. For example, a study might compare how non-governmental organizations (NGOs) are operating in a particular region of a country and also contrast their interpretations of a policy to those of the NGO directors in the capital or to the NGOs' donors in another country. This is a quite different conceptualization of replication design as promoted by Yin and the need for tightly bounded units of analysis that it implies. However, writing about how processes unfold in unpredictable ways across space and time often proves to be more challenging than resorting back to descriptions of multiple cases juxtaposed with one another. Through the examples of CCSs in the chapters to follow, we illustrate how, nonetheless, this can be done.

Another feature of the CCS approach is that it aims to understand and incorporate, at least partially, the perspectives of social actors in the study. This is common to most qualitative research, especially ethnography and ethnographically-oriented studies. As Willis and Trondman stated, ethnography (and, we would add, other qualitative methods) are "a family of methods involving direct and sustained social contact with agents and of richly writing up the encounter, respecting, recording, representing *at least partly in its own terms* the irreducibility of human experience" (2000, p. 394, emphasis ours).

The CCS approach is also informed by a critical theoretical stance. By critical, we mean that the approach is guided by critical theory and its concerns and assumptions regarding power and inequality. Drawing upon Marxist, feminist, and critical race theory, among others, critical theory aims to critique inequality and change society; it studies the cultural production of structures, processes, and practices of power, exploitation, and agency; and it reveals how common-sense, hegemonic notions about the social world maintain disparities of various sorts.[3]

Attention to power and inequality is central to the CCS approach, meaning it would be difficult for researchers with distinctly different epistemological loyalties to engage it fully. For instance, many interpretivist scholars focus only on local meanings and symbolic systems while downplaying the historical, material, and structural forces that allow some groups to have greater influence over dominant meanings and representations. Some reject comparison as a worthwhile strategy because their interpretivist approach leads them to emphasize thickly describing a single case. We also see a variance orientation as a poor fit for our version of case study research because its nomothetic stance implies a search for regularities or law-like generalizations that provide the basis for causal explanation and prediction. But human behavior and continuous cultural production are unpredictable. Further, this approach doesn't address the "how" or "why" questions, which are fundamental to process-oriented case studies.

In addition to these features of the CCS approach, we have developed it as a way to 'unbound' culture while still seeking to conduct rich descriptions of the phenomenon of interest to the researcher. This is particularly important in policy studies, and we consider the CCS approach to be highly productive for the exploration of the cultural politics of policy as it plays out at multiple scales. CCS calls on researchers to think about how they might achieve cultural understanding of the production and appropriation of policy by doing shorter-term periods of research in multiple sites across different scales to create a case study attentive to horizontal, vertical, and temporal comparison. The examples provided in this book demonstrate the possibility of such an approach that remains focused on cultural politics and production.

Finally, we argue that both neo-positivist and interpretivist case study approaches miss a major opportunity by not integrating comparison more centrally into their work. Our processual approach to comparison considers strings of relevant events and actors; it eschews staid notions of culture or context to consider those processes *across space and time*; and it *constantly compares* what is happening in one locale with what has happened in other places and historical moments. These forms of comparison are what we herein call horizontal, vertical, and transversal comparisons.

In this next section, we elaborate the conceptual underpinnings of our CCS approach, which is particularly influenced by extended case methods, multi-sited ethnography, and actor network theory.

Theorizing the CCS Approach

One of the main challenges of contemporary social research is to resolve, or at least address, the realization that local sociocultural action is shaped by larger social, political, and economic structures and processes. Central to our understanding of the local/global dilemma has been Anna Tsing's theorization of "global connections" (2005, p. 1). As Tsing wrote, seemingly global and universalizing systems, such as capitalism and democracy, operate in specific material and social contexts. These systems "can only be charged and enacted in the *sticky materiality of practical encounters*" (p. 3, emphasis ours). These so-called global forces, she contended, are themselves "congeries" of local-global interactions. To illustrate the study of global connections, Tsing introduced the metaphor of friction. She argued that friction is produced through continuous social interaction among actors at various levels and is required to "keep global power in motion," though it may just as easily "slow things down" (p. 6). This metaphor encapsulates "the awkward, unequal, unstable, and creative qualities of interconnection across difference" (p. 6). Global encounters, when conceptualized in this way, often result in new and unanticipated cultural and political forms that exclude as well as enable.

Understanding how globalization shapes and is culturally produced in social life, then, requires simultaneous attention to multiple levels, including (at least) international, national, and local ones, and careful study of flows (and frictions) of influence, ideas, and actions through these levels. Qualitative research must consider the profound changes in the global economy and (inter) national politics that make the national and international levels of analysis as important as the local. The growing interconnections between national economies and international financial institutions, and between national educational and social service systems and global organizations that fund and evaluate their operations, are some of the most important issues for scholars today.

Comparative case studies examine these interconnections by de-centering the nation-state from its privileged position as *the* fundamental entity in comparative research and relocating it as one of several important units of analysis. As Marginson and Mollis (2001) wrote: "Governance remains national in form, and nation-states continue to be central players in a globalizing world, but partly as local agents of global forces, [as] the nation-state now operates within global economic constraints" (p. 601). Thus, multi-level research that situates the nation-state within a world marked by global agencies and agendas is essential. Yet the national–global relationship is only one part of a comparative case study because the local–national and the local–global connections are equally significant. The goal of CCS research is to develop a thorough understanding of the particular at each scale and to analyze how these understandings produce similar and different interpretations of the policy, problem, or phenomenon under study.

This reconceptualization of globalization parallels other conceptual developments that have influenced our methodological approach, including extended case methods, multi-sited ethnography, and actor network theory, as outlined below.

Extended Case Method

Our conceptualization of the CCS approach builds upon the extended case method. This approach, rooted in work conducted by anthropologists Max Gluckman and Jaap van Velsen in the late 1950s and early 1960s, has been developed by sociologist Michael Burawoy (1991, 1998, 2009). To counter the excesses of both positivism and interpretivism, including decontextualized abstractions regarding social structures, the extended case method emphasizes individual strategies and tactics in everyday life. The edited collection of case studies, suggestively called *Ethnography Unbound* (Burawoy, 1991), paired chapters that are each based on intensive participation in the same metropolis, focused on different topics, as a means of comparing the ethnographic cases; each chapter included an insightful reflection on research dilemmas. The chapters drew on critical theory in order to compare how "everyday life in the modern metropolis is continually eroded, distorted, overpowered by, and subordinated to institutional forces that seem beyond human control" (p. 1) and to identify a range of strategies of resistance. Specifically, the extended case method consists of four distinct dimensions: participant observation or "the extension of the observer into the world of the participant" (Burawoy, 2000, p. 26); the extension of observations "over time and space," with care to diversify participants; "extending out from micro processes to macro forces"; and the "extension of theory," often by using cases to critique existing theory and develop alternative hypotheses (pp. 14–37).

The CCS approach draws on the extended case method in several ways. These include its embrace of critical theory; the opportunities to generalize, theoretically rather than statistically, from qualitative work; and the comparing of theoretically similar work done on different topics in different places (within or beyond the same city). However, we diverge from Burawoy in important ways as well. For instance, more contemporary theoretical work allows us to engage more processual, less static notions of cultural processes. We strive to avoid engaging a sense of (economic and power) structures as apart from, and impinging on, local practices. In addition, we seek to encourage thinking about the social production of space and place, as well as relations across scales.

Multi-Sited and Multi-Scalar Ethnography and the Spatial Turn

Among qualitative social scientists, research approaches have become increasingly multi-sited over the past 20 years. While techniques for engaging multiple field sites have existed for quite some time and were used intensively by urban anthropologists in the 1960s and those working transnationally in the 1990s, multi-sited ethnography has been most coherently codified in the work of George Marcus (1995, 1998). Marcus (1995) described this work as "mobile ethnography [that] takes unexpected trajectories in tracing a cultural formation across and within multiple sites of activity" (p. 96). As further explained by Falzon (2009):

> The essence of multi-sited research is to follow people, connections, associations, and relationships across space (because they *are substantially continuous but spatially non-contiguous*) .... Research design proceeds by a series of *juxtapositions* in which the global is collapsed into and made an integral part of parallel, related local situations, rather than something monolithic or external to them. In terms of method, multi-sited ethnography involves a *spatially dispersed field* through which the ethnographer moves.
>
> (pp. 1–2, emphasis ours)

Thus, multi-sited ethnography requires what we are calling a tracing across space (and, we would add, time) of a "spatially dispersed field." It entails the rejection of the notion of holism, which implies discrete and timeless cultures, and the reconceptualization of context to include a sense of places as socially produced across scales. Multi-sited ethnography was spurred by recognition of not only the flow of people, goods, and ideas across space but also the inter-connectedness across dispersed locations and the larger political economic framework (Coleman & von Hellermann, 2011; Marcus, 1986). In addition, it addresses the necessity of examining "distributed knowledge systems" and "active knowledge making," or the multiple and spatially diffused sources of knowledge and ways of knowing among those participating in ethnographic studies (Coleman & von Hellermann, 2011, pp. 23–25). Marcus outlined several possible tracking strategies, including following the people, the thing, the metaphor, the plot, the life history, and the conflict (1995).

Others have weighed in on multi-sited ethnographic research strategies. As Hannerz (2003) argued, the effort to trace a problem across locations is not simply "multi-sited":

> In a way, one might argue, the term 'multilocal' is a little misleading, for what current multilocal projects have in common is that they draw on some problem, some formulation of a topic, which is significantly translo-cal, not to be confined within some single place. The sites are connected with one another in such ways that *the relationships between them are as important for this formulation as the relationships within them*; the fields are not some mere collection of local units. One must establish the translo-cal linkages, and the interconnections between those and whatever local bundles of relationships which are also part of the study ....
>
> (Hannerz, 2003, p. 206, emphasis ours)

This sense of "translocal" suggests one part of what we try to attain in the CCS approach. Our emphasis on 'tracing' emphasizes the 'relationships between' sites. These may not be known from the outside of the study, and are discovered through the data collection process. Yet, the CCS approach reconceptualizes and recasts the notion of translocal in three ways: (1) expecting multiple sites of study at a single scale (through horizontal comparison); (2) examining what they have in common by looking at national or international policymaking (through vertical comparison); and (3) exploring how these horizontal and vertical connections were formed historically and have led to spatially differentiated effects (transversal comparison). For example, to study the issue of school vouchers in Milwaukee might require participant observation within several schools and their concomitant "communities," however conceived; interviews at the city and state legislature; a document analysis of relevant policies; interviews and archival work in the teachers' union; and a consideration of national educational policy politics, as well as political economic forces. Such efforts shift "locales" and "levels";

they entail attention across sites and require multiple research techniques. Some of these will be more central to the study, and others will provide the backdrop for it.

The CCS approach also entails systematic comparison. Hannerz argued that multi-sited work differs from *"a mere comparative study of localities* (which in one classical mode of anthropological comparison was based precisely on the assumption that such linkages did not exist)" (2003, p. 206). Here, we diverge from him; with our emphasis on horizontal comparison, we argue that much can be learned from contrasting sites. But we also take his point that linkages should be an important focus. Hannerz continued, explaining that "site selections are to an extent made *gradually and cumulatively*, as new insights develop, as opportunities come into sight, and to some extent by chance" (2003, pp. 206–207, emphasis ours). This description of the gradual and cumulative selection of sites is what we herein describe as a contingent and iterative tracing of relevant factors, actors, and features. By contingent, we mean that the research design must respond to regularly evolving cultural, political, and material conditions of the work, as well as data collected. By iterative, we explicitly reference Maxwell (2013), who urged qualitative researchers to eschew linear approaches, which provide a prescriptive guide for completing tasks. Instead, he recommended an interactive, iterative approach, in which researchers remain flexible throughout the research process, consider the implications of data collection and analysis for conceptual frames, research questions, and research design, and regularly change the design plan in response.

Furthermore, this shift in qualitative research results from a reconceptualization of space as socially produced. Massey suggested that we think of space as "the product of interrelations ... constituted through interactions ... always under construction" (2005, p. 9; see also de Certeau, 1984). This "spatial turn" requires a rethinking of the global/local antinomy (e.g. Kearney, 1995), moving away from the tendency to look at how global structures shape local practices and toward a recognition that seemingly universalizing systems, which include policy regimes, "can only be charged and enacted in the sticky materiality of practical encounters" (Tsing, 2005, p. 3). This shift triggers what Feldman (2011) called "the decomposition of ethnographic location," particularly at a time when the idea of the "culture" or "social group" as a unit of study has been heavily critiqued (p. 377). Globalization and transnationalism "challenge ethnographic methods of inquiry and units of analysis by destabilizing the embeddedness of social relations in particular communities and places" (Falzon, 2009, p. 2). This challenge calls for new methodological approaches, such as the ones we propose here.

The notion of "scale" prompts a slight rethinking of multi-sited ethnography, producing what anthropologist Biao Xiang called "multi-scalar ethnography" (2013). In his study of migration in and from China, Xiang employed multi-scalar ethnography, which considers how social phenomena are *"constituted* through actions at different scales" (p. 284). As Xiang expounded, smooth flows at one scale (e.g. international) can be disruptive at another (e.g. family or community). At the same time, smooth transnational flows may not be possible without the deep disruptions in family or the tight encapsulations of individual life.

(p. 282)

For example, migrants' efforts to reshape their economic and social lives intersect with the state's "scale management" and disrupt family life. Social actors of various sorts engage in "scale-making," or developing and sustaining understandings of different scales and projecting possible futures (e.g., Marston, 2000; Nespor, 2004). Further, Tsing (2000) cautioned that we must pay attention to how beliefs and claims about scales—e.g., the local or the global—function. Because scales are, in part, culturally produced, they are unpredictable and open to change. They require iterative methods to trace scale-making.

They also require critical awareness. Xiang (2013) cautioned that researchers must be reflexive about their own scalar positionality and how it is influencing data collection and analysis. Scale influences what we see, exerting a telescopic or accordion effect. As Ingold (2010) wrote, phenomena "can be observed at different scales, from close up to far away, and each will reveal different patterns, textures, and grains" (p. 125). Furthermore, as Hastrup has emphasized, "The act of scaling is a matter of putting a particular perspective to work—it unsettles the idea of the stationary anthropological object of observation and the holism upon which anthropology was premised" (2013, p. 148; see also Latour, 2005). It is up to the researcher to document methodological decisions about what to pursue, and why, and to maintain a critical reflexivity about that process and its impact on the findings.

Multi-sited and multi-scalar ethnography remind us of the importance of considering different scales, their (occasionally harmonious, often disruptive) intersections, and their mutual cultural production. These approaches encourage us to track or trace *across and through* sites and scales. To conceptualize that work, we draw on actor network theory, as outlined in the next section.

Actor Network Theory

Comparative case studies can be further enhanced by concepts derived from actor network theory (ANT), which offers a conceptual and methodological approach to the notion of studying across and through. Networks are "assemblages" of dynamic actors and resources that can "move educational practices across space and time" (Nespor, 2003, p. 369; Ong & Collier, 2005). As developed by Latour (2005) and others, ANT considers how, within networks, people and objects get invited, excluded, and enrolled, a moment in which they accept (at least temporarily) the interests and agenda as set by focal actors; how linkages are established (or fail to 'take'), shift, and dissolve;

and how social acts curtail or facilitate future actions. Koyama (2011), as discussed in Chapter 4, explained:

> The strength of the theory lies in its insistence on following the ongoing processes 'made up of uncertain, fragile, controversial, and ever-shifting ties' (Latour, 2005, p. 28) rather than attempting to fit the actors and their activities into bounded categories, geographical sites, or groups of analysis.
>
> (p. 705)

In this way, ANT directly contravenes the injunction in contemporary case study methodologies to "bound the case."

Importantly, and quite controversially, ANT emphasizes the role played by non-human actors, which, in effect, dissolves binaries by focusing on *interactions* among actors within a network rather than on their location (local, national, global) within it. From this perspective, people, objects, and texts can become vested and act, and ANT traces how human and non-human actors become "enrolled" in and are then "accountable" to networks, and how both are "produced by particular interactions with one another" (Fenwick & Edwards, 2010, p. 8).

Comparative case studies examine spatially non-contiguous assemblages of actors across scales. For example, in her study of climate change in the Arctic, anthropologist Kirsten Hastrup (2013) explained how discussions and activities draw from numerous places, diverse epochs, and reigning discourses. Her fieldwork in northwest Greenland "addresses the question of scaling through discussions of conversations, connections and concerns surfacing in the field, yet vastly transcending the local" (p. 145). At one moment, focusing on the impact of climate change on the ice, she wrote that participants' "connections are circumscribed by forces of nature that are becoming increasingly unpredictable" (p. 155). Hastrup eloquently explained how this bold new type of fieldwork redefines the very notion of *field*:

> Field itself [is] a plastic space, where the fieldworker's attention may stretch and bend according to situation and perspective …. *Fields are as emergent as are anthropological interests, which is one reason for fieldwork being a mutable and endlessly challenging practice.* To have 'enough' ethnographic material is not a simple function of the long term, but more of the questions asked …. The field itself comes in many shapes and sizes, because it emerges through different perspectives.
>
> (2013, pp. 145–146, emphasis ours)

Fieldwork, she continued, must follow "the connections that are traceable prior to any attempt at summing up the ingredients of the whole" (Hastrup, 2013, p. 157).

Drawing on such insights, we develop several tenets for the CCS heuristic. First, adequate case studies are not merely a question of time in the field but of the quality of the questions posed and the methods used to address them. Second, a comparative case study cannot be "bounded" from the start of the study. Fields are emergent, and fieldwork is mutable. A comparative case study looks across scales and consider how scales intersect, through a process of inquiry that follows the phenomenon. Actor network theory provides one feasible conceptual and methodological approach, but we seek to enhance it in several ways. We not only emphasize tracing across similar cases, but we also value the inclusion of cases that are quite distinct and generate insights via juxtaposition. The notion of tracing runs the risk of ignoring the potential benefits of contrastive cases. Further, by emphasizing the transversal axis, the CCS heuristic explicitly promotes historical comparison.

Exercise 2.3 Playing with Key Concepts

The research questions that you are working with suggest a particular design, and we assume that if you are reading this book, you are giving some thought to conducting a comparative case study. If so, this is a good time to imagine the kind of study you might want to carry out to address your tentative research questions.

- Using these three key concepts, write a few sentences about how your study could be: (1) multi-sited; (2) multi-scalar; and could utilize (3) actor network theory.
- This is also an ideal time to start diagramming—making mental maps—of your study on a whiteboard or on some other space where you can make frequent changes to your emerging design. The point is not to choose sites, scales, and actors that you must include in your study; the goal at this point is to think creatively and expansively at this point in the development of your project.

Conclusion

In this chapter, we examined and critiqued several existing models of case study research. We problematized the notion of boundedness, in particular, and we also reconsidered notions of context and culture as they are used in the traditional case study literature. We argued that context should not be defined as place or location, but it should rather be conceptualized as something spatial and relational. We also explained why we eschew a static, bounded notion of culture in favor of a view of culture as an ongoing, contested production. These notions are consequential for how we conceptualize case studies and comparison, as we illustrate in the remainder of the book. Finally, the chapter showed how the CCS approach has been shaped by our reading of work on the extended case method, multi-sited and multi-scalar ethnography, and actor network theory. In the next three chapters, we elaborate on the CCS approach by taking up each of the three central axes—the horizontal, the vertical, and the transversal—in turn and illustrating their use with studies by doctoral students and more established scholars.

Notes

1 Using a related term, Ragin elaborated:

> "[I]n most variable-oriented research, investigators begin by defining the prob-
> lem in a way that allows examination of many cases (conceived as empirical
> units or observations); then they specify the relevant variables, matched to
> theoretical concepts; and finally they collect information on these variables,
> usually one variable at a time—not one case at a time. From that point on, the
> language of variables and the relationships among them dominate the research
> process. The resulting understanding of these relations is shaped by examining
> patterns of covariation in the data set, observed and averaged across many cases,
> not by studying how different features or causes fit together in individual cases.
> (1992, p. 5)

2 To be fair, Yin does acknowledge that the design may change over time. He wrote:

> [W]hen you do eventually arrive at the definition of the unit of analysis, do not
> consider closure permanent. Your choice of the unit of analysis, as with other
> facets of your research design, can be revisited as a result of discoveries during
> your data collection.
> (2011, pp. 31–32)

3 It is important to distinguish our use of critical from two other uses that appear in
the case study literature. Patton (1990) denominated *critical cases* as "those that
can make a point quite dramatically or are, for some reason, particularly important
in the scheme of things" (p. 174). Critical, for Patton, denoted a somewhat typical case—"if it happens there, it will happen anywhere." In this sense, a "critical"
case has strategic importance in relation to the problem, allowing generalization, or
(in contrast) providing for falsification by showing that general claims are invalid
for this case (and, potentially, similar cases). A second notion of the term, what is
called "critical incident case study," considers the factors, variables, or behaviors
that are "critical to the success or failure of an activity or event and associated
outcomes" (p. 247). With its focus on events, the method considers the "causal
antecedents of an event and those critical actions or inactions taken by actors or
agents that contributed to the event's or outcome's occurrence" (p. 247).

References

Appadurai, A. (1996). *Modernity at large: Cultural dimensions of globalization.*
Minneapolis: University of Minnesota Press.

Becker, H. S. (2009). How to find out how to do qualitative research. *International
Journal of Communication 3*, 545–553.

Burawoy, M. (1991). *Ethnography unbound: Power and resistance in the modern metropolis.* Berkeley: University of California Press.

Burawoy, M. (1998). The extended case method. *Sociological Theory 16*, 4–33.

Burawoy, M. (2000). Introduction: Reaching for the global. In M. Burawoy et al.
(Eds.), *Global ethnography: Forces, connections and imaginations in a postmodern world*
(pp. 1–40). Berkeley: University of California Press.

Burawoy, M. (2009). *The extended case method: Four countries, four decades, four great
transformations, and one theoretical tradition.* Berkeley: University of California Press.

Coleman, S., & von Hellermann, P. (Eds.). (2011). *Multi-sited ethnography: Problems
and possibilities in the translocation of research methods.* New York: Routledge.

Creswell, J. (2013). *Research design: Qualitative, quantitative, and mixed methods approaches.* Thousand Oaks, CA: Sage.

de Certeau, M. (1984). *The practice of everyday life.* Berkeley: University of California Press.

Falzon, M. (2009). Introduction. In M. Falzon (Ed.), *Multi-sited ethnography: Theory, praxis and locality in contemporary research* (pp. 1–24). Aldershot, UK: Ashgate.

Feldman, G. (2011). If ethnography is more than participant-observation, then relations are more than connections: The case for nonlocal ethnography in a world of apparatuses. *Anthropological Theory 11*(4), 375–395.

Fenwick, T., & Edwards, R. (2010). *Actor-network theory in education.* New York: Routledge.

Flyvberg, B. (2011). Case study. In N. K. Denzin & Y. S. Lincoln (Eds.), *The handbook of qualitative research* (4th ed.) (pp. 301–316). Thousand Oaks, CA: Sage.

Geertz, C. (1973). *The interpretation of cultures.* New York: Basic Books.

Gomm, R., Hammersley, M., & Foster, P. (2000). Case study and generalization. In R. Gomm, M. Hammersley, & P. Foster (Eds.), *Case study method* (pp. 98–115). London: Sage.

Guba, E. G., & Lincoln, Y. S. (1994). Competing paradigms in qualitative research. In N. K. Denzin & Y. S. Lincoln (Eds.), *The handbook of qualitative research* (pp. 105–117). Thousand Oaks, CA: Sage.

Hannerz, U. (2003). Being there... and there... and there! Reflections on multi-site ethnography. *Ethnography 4*(2), 201–216.

Hastrup, K. (2013). Scales of attention in fieldwork: Global connections and local concerns in the Arctic. *Ethnography 14*(2), 145–164.

Heath, S. B., & Street, B. (2008). *On ethnography: Approaches to language and literacy research.* New York: Teachers College Press.

Ingold, T. (2010). Footprints through the weather-world: Walking, breathing, knowing. *Journal of the Royal Anthropological Institute,* S121–S139.

Kearney, M. (1995). The local and the global: The anthropology of globalization and transnationalism. *Annual Reviews in Anthropology 24*(1), 547–565.

Koyama, J. (2011). Generating, comparing, manipulating, categorizing, reporting, and sometimes fabricating data to comply with No Child Left Behind mandates. *Journal of Education Policy 26*(5), 701–720.

Latour, B. (2005). *Reassembling the social: An introduction to actor-network theory.* Oxford: Oxford University Press.

Lincoln, Y. S., & Guba, E. G. (1985). *Naturalistic inquiry.* Beverly Hills, CA: Sage.

Lincoln, Y. S., & Guba, E. G. (1986). But is it rigorous? Trustworthiness and authenticity in naturalistic evaluation. In D. D. Williams (Ed.), *Naturalistic evaluation* (pp. 73–84). San Francisco: Jossey-Bass.

Marcus, G. E. (1986). Contemporary problems of ethnography in the modern world system. In J. Clifford & G. E. Marcus (Eds.), *Writing culture: The poetics and politics of ethnography* (pp. 165–193). Berkeley: University of California Press.

Marcus, G. E. (1995). Ethnography in/of the world system: The emergence of multi-sited ethnography. *Annual Review of Anthropology 24*, 95–117.

Marcus, G. E. (1998). *Ethnography through thick and thin.* Princeton, NJ: Princeton University Press.

Marginson, S., & Mollis, M. (2001). "The door opens and the tiger leaps": Theories and reflexivities of comparative education for a global millennium. *Comparative Education Review 45*(4), 581–615.

Marston, S. (2000). The social construction of scale. *Progress in Human Geography 24*(2), 219–242.

Massey, D. (2005) *For space*. London: Sage.

Maxwell, J. A. (2004). Causal explanation, qualitative research, and scientific inquiry in education. *Educational Researcher 33*(2), 3–11.

Maxwell, J. A. (2013). *Qualitative research design: An interactive approach* (3rd ed.). Thousand Oaks, CA: Sage.

Merriam, S. B. (1998). *Qualitative research and case study applications in education*. San Francisco: Jossey-Bass.

Miles, M. B., & Huberman, A. M. (1994). *Qualitative data analysis: An expanded sourcebook*. Thousand Oaks, CA: Sage.

Nespor, J. (2003). *Networks and contexts of reform*. Blacksburg, VA: Virginia Polytechnic Institute & State University.

Nespor, J. (2004). Educational scale-making. *Pedagogy, Culture & Society 12*(3), 309–326.

Ong, A., & Collier, S. J. (Eds.). (2005). *Global assemblages: Technology, politics and ethics as anthropological problems*. Malden, MA: Blackwell.

O'Reilly, K. (2009). *Key concepts in ethnography*. Thousand Oaks, CA: Sage.

Patton, M. Q. (1990). *Qualitative research and evaluation: Integrating theory and practice* (2nd ed.). Thousand Oaks, CA: Sage.

Ragin, C. C. (1992). Introduction: Cases of "what is a case?" In C. Ragin & H. S. Becker (Eds.), *What is a case? Exploring the foundations of social inquiry* (pp. 1–17). New York: Cambridge University Press.

Stake, R. E. (1994). Case studies. In N. K. Denzin & Y. S. Lincoln (Eds.), *Handbook of qualitative research* (pp. 236–247). Thousand Oaks, CA: Sage.

Stake, R. E. (1995). *The art of case study research*. Thousand Oaks, CA: Sage.

Stake, R. E. (2003). Case studies. In N. K. Denzin & Y. S. Lincoln (Eds.), *Strategies of qualitative inquiry* (2nd ed.) (pp. 134–164). Thousand Oaks, CA: Sage.

Stake, R. E. (2006). *Multiple case study analysis*. New York: The Guilford Press.

Trochim, W. M. (2006). *The research methods knowledge base* (2nd ed.). Retrieved from http://www.socialresearchmethods.net/kb/.

Tsing, A. (2000). The global situation. *Cultural Anthropology 15*(3), 327–360.

Tsing, A. L. (2005). *Friction: An ethnography of global connections*. Princeton, NJ: Princeton University Press.

van der Veer, P. (2016). *The value of comparison*. Durham, NC: Duke University Press.

Wherry, F. (2015). Fragments from an ethnographer's field guide: Skepticism, thick minimalism, and big theory. *Ethnography*. DOI: 10.1177/1466138115592422

Willis, P., & Trondman, M. (2000). Manifesto for ethnography. *Ethnography 1*(1), 5–16.

Xiang, B. (2013). Multi-scalar ethnography: An approach for critical engagement with migration and social change. *Ethnography 14*(3), 282–299.

Yin, R. K. (1994). *Case study research: Design and methods* (2nd ed.). Thousand Oaks, CA: Sage.

Yin, R. K. (2009). *Case study research: Design and methods* (4th ed.). Thousand Oaks, CA: Sage.

Yin, R. K. (2011). *Applications of case study research*. Thousand Oaks, CA: Sage.

Yin, R. K. (2014). *Case study research: Design and methods* (5th ed.). Thousand Oaks, CA: Sage.

3   Horizontal Comparison

In his 2013 Lewis Henry Morgan lecture "The Value of Comparison," anthropologist Peter van der Veer addressed the thorny question of how best to wrest analytical purchase from comparison. He criticized the tendency to oversimplify cases, as well as the habit of ignoring how similar historical or contemporary social factors influence cases. He was particularly critical of Euro-American social science and the constant, facile juxtapositions of 'the West' and 'the Other.' He wrote:

> The pervasiveness of ethnocentrism in the social sciences is astonishing …. One of the greatest flaws in the development of a comparative perspective seems to be the almost universal comparison of any existing society with an ideal-typical and totally self-sufficient Euro-American modernity. Comparison should not be conceived primarily in terms of comparing societies or events, or institutional arrangements across societies, although this is important, but *as a reflection on our conceptual framework as well as on the history of interactions that have constituted our object of study. Comparison is thus not a relatively simple juxtaposition and comparison of two or more different societies, but a complex reflection on the network of concepts that underlie our study of society as well as the formation of those societies themselves. It is always a double act of reflection.*
> (2013, pp. 3–4, emphasis ours; see also van der Veer, 2016)

We begin with this quote from van der Veer because the aim of this chapter is to explain our conceptualization of the horizontal axis in the comparative case study (CCS) approach and demonstrate how to conduct such work with several illustrative examples. Like van der Veer, we seek to avoid the imposition of *a priori* categories derived from one place, scholarly tradition, or group onto another, which often occurs when one is comparing horizontally. The *processual approach to comparison* that we have introduced in the previous chapters provides a strategy for meeting these goals because it shows how one can compare the way that similar phenomena unfold in distinct, socially-produced locations that are connected in multiple and complex ways.

In this chapter, we will discuss two approaches to horizontal comparison: the homologous and the heterologous. By homologous, we mean the entities being compared have a corresponding position or structure to one another, such as three classrooms in one high school, or two clinics that provide services to pregnant women. For example, Denise Pope's (2001) comparative study followed, for one year, five academically high-achieving American youth who were experiencing high levels of stress. To a lesser degree, Annette Lareau's study (2011) (discussed below) of parenting strategies marked by social class focused primarily at the level of family. Homologous studies compare and contrast, thinking carefully about how similar forces (e.g., a policy, or an economic trend, or a program) result in similar and different practices, and why. Though some projects emphasize connection, many are often driven by a logic of *juxtaposition*. These studies tend to be more pre-structured, though they too remain open to innovation. Scholars may use a specific sampling strategy (such as maximum variation or most similar cases) to initially select their cases; however, as the study unfolds, they may add new cases, or abandon cases they originally thought would be useful.

Further, homologous comparative cases may or may not involve "nested" or "embedded" comparisons, which integrate a vertical element by situating the homologous units within a broader study at a different scale.[1] For instance, nested studies might consider the implementation of a new curriculum in two schools per district in three districts, or the impact of a new health care policy in five clinics per municipality in two provinces, or how community policing is implemented in different neighborhoods across three cities.

In contrast, by heterologous, we mean entities that are categorically distinct, such as a school, a clinic, and an NGO, but are important in the unfolding of the phenomenon of interest. For example, the sociologist Matthew Desmond (2016) followed processes of eviction as he moved through trailer parks, public housing units, eviction courts, shelters, abandoned houses, churches, funerals, and AA meetings in a single city, Milwaukee. Though they may entail juxtaposition, the logic behind heterologous horizontal comparison is usually one of *connection*; it entails tracing a phenomenon across a "spatially dispersed" social field (Falzon, 2009, p. 1). This approach requires some sociological detective work, thinking broadly about the wide variety of factors, forces, and actions that shape a social problem, and the sites in which the problem is culturally produced. This is the sort of tracing we referenced in Chapter 1, when we quoted James Ferguson's (2012) assertion that, to understand violence in Nigeria's oil-rich delta region, an analyst would need to consider a network of factors, including local politics, land tenure, ethnic formations, and NGO work, among other things. In such a study, the researcher may begin with a set of 'clues' to follow, but many sites of study will be identified as the study unfolds. Heterologous comparison is often found in multi-sited ethnographies, as discussed in the previous chapter and in Examples 3.4 and 3.5 in this chapter. This kind of multi-sited, heterologous, emergent comparison is a hallmark of contemporary ethnographies in the field of anthropology (e.g., Falzon, 2009; Reichman, 2011;

Roy, 2010). Notably, sites that are relevant to the phenomenon of interest may well be at different scales, thus blending with the vertical axis (for more on this, see Chapter 4). Indeed, we champion studies that work across the three axes of the horizontal, the vertical, and the transversal when feasible.

A number of research methods can be used to develop the horizontal axis of a CCS, whether one uses a homologous or heterologous logic in site selection. In this chapter, we discuss interviews and observations because they are particularly well suited for horizontal comparison, though they may be used in the vertical and transversal axes as well, as discussed in Chapters 4 and 5. We then examine several comparative case studies based on books and dissertations to illustrate how horizontal comparison can benefit the study of policy, education, and other topics. The first example is taken from Lareau's *Unequal Childhoods* (2011), a comparative study of childhoods and parenting strategies. The second is Bethany Wilinski's (2014) study of pre-kindergarten for four-year olds (4K) in Wisconsin, titled '*I Don't Want PreK to Turn into School': What PreK Policy Means in Practice*. The third is Michele Bellino's dissertation, *Memory in Transition: Historical Consciousness and Civic Attitudes among Youth in 'Postwar' Guatemala* (2014). We then use two examples to illustrate heterologous horizontal comparison: Nancy Kendall's book, *The Sex Education Debates*, a multi-sited ethnography of sex education in the United States (2012), and Monisha Bajaj's (2012) *Schooling for Social Change*, a study of human rights education in India. However, before turning to these techniques and examples, we outline the central assumptions that inform horizontal comparison.

Horizontal Comparison: Central Assumptions

The horizontal axis is informed by both traditional comparative case studies and by multi-sited ethnography, as described in Chapter 2. From these areas of inquiry, we derive a few central assumptions that inform our development of horizontal comparison:

- Horizontal comparison requires attention to how historical and contemporary processes have differentially influenced different 'cases,' which might be defined as people, groups of people, sites, institutions, social movements, partnerships, etc.
- Horizontal comparisons avoid imposing categories that are derived solely from one case onto another.
- The inclusion of multiple cases at the same scale in a comparative case study need not flatten the cases by ignoring valuable contextual information about each one.
- Homologous horizontal comparisons use units of analysis that are fairly equivalent (e.g., schools, medical clinics, or states). Though such studies may be more structured than heterologous comparisons, they too must alter case inclusion according to emergent findings.

- Homologous comparative cases may or may not involve "nested" or "embedded" comparisons, which integrate a vertical element.
- Heterologous comparative case studies entail tracing a phenomenon across sites, as in multi-sited ethnography. It is important to consider sites that may be more or less the same scale but may not be categorically equivalent.

Having identified these premises, we now turn to a discussion of interviews and observations. We then look at how these methods have been used in several exemplary studies.

Methods for Developing the Horizontal Axis

There are many research methods that can be used to develop the horizontal axis in a comparative case study. For example, a study might involve surveys or focus groups. However, we have found that interviews and observations are two of the most important methods. This is because rich description of each horizontal element—each theater program, each teacher, each partnership—is critical to discerning the similarities and differences across the sites. In what follows, we give a brief overview of the method and emphasize how it can be used in horizontal comparisons.

Interviews

Interviews are a fundamental research method in the humanities and social sciences. They provide an opportunity for more or less structured in-depth conversations with diverse social actors and help researchers to get a sense of these actors' reported experiences and differing perspectives on the phenomenon of interest. They also allow participants to expose ambivalences or mixed reactions to events, a policy, or more informal rules of conduct in an organization.

Interview formats range, depending on the epistemological stance and goals of the project. In a structured interview, the questions are predetermined and fixed; the interviewer generally does not add, delete, or even reorder questions. This style imposes categories and concepts that structure the project and produces more standardized interviews across interviewers (e.g., on a research team) and interviewees, thus, in some ways, facilitating direct comparison. Structured interviews also require the researcher to maintain control of the interaction, and this is one reason why structured interviews are most common in survey research, where standardization of questions and controlled interactions between the researcher and the interviewee are considered necessary to obtain putatively unbiased responses (see Chapter 5 for more details on survey research).

In contrast, unstructured interviews are more free-flowing. The researcher likely has a list of topics or broad questions to cover but gives the interviewee extensive control over how the conversation develops. The interview is highly flexible, allowing conversation participants to follow or drop topics, or pursue new topics, as they emerge. Finally, an interview might be semi-structured, which combines the first two approaches: Questions are often prepared in advance but with flexibility in the ordering and the actual wording of the questions, and the researcher maintains more control over the conversation but allows for some spontaneous back-and-forth between the researcher and the interviewee (O'Reilly, 2005, 2009).

Semi-structured and unstructured interviews are more consistent with the CCS approach because they more fully attend to the processural nature of conversation and the social dimensions of knowledge production. However, structured interviews can also be useful in certain instances, especially if there is a group of participants in your study whose time might be very limited or who are unlikely to disclose their opinions in any detail. For example, if you are interested in the phenomenon of residential redlining, or denying services to a specific group (often defined by geography or ethnicity), then you might have a very structured interview protocol to use with realtors whose institutions are known to have engaged in redlining. In the same study, you might have a semi-structured interview guide for realtors whose institutions arose to counter redlining. The first part of the semi-structured interview protocol might be identical to the structured one for the 'redlining realtors,' but the second part would contain semi-structured or even open-ended questions that would facilitate the sharing of experiences by those who started real estate companies to thwart redlining. In addition, a researcher might choose to do one type of interview during one phase or stage of research and a different type at a different phase. For example, in the longitudinal study of secondary schooling in Tanzania that Frances Vavrus discusses in Chapter 5, she used a semi-structured interview protocol in 2007 with youth in the study but opted for progressively less-structured interview guides in subsequent interviews as these youth grew into young adults.

Social researchers often fail to think about who they are selecting to interview and why. Sometimes, snowball sampling (where the researcher interviews someone, and asks her to recommend a second person, then interview the second person, and again ask for others to interview) or convenience sampling (where the researcher interviews those who are easiest or most convenient to reach) are the only options available. However, when feasible, we encourage you to think specifically about who you want to interview, how (e.g., structured or not), about what, and why—and to document these decisions.

A multitude of books and articles offer helpful guidance on how to develop an interview guide and improve one's interviewing skills (e.g., Heyl, 2001; Kvale, 1996; LeCompte & Schensul, 2010; LeCompte & Preissle, 2003; May, 2001; O'Reilly, 2005; Rubin & Rubin, 1995; Seidman, 2013). All of these sources address the importance of thinking carefully about the content of interview guides. Patton (2001) suggested the following categories for the types of questions that researchers might ask depending on the kinds of data they seek to gather through interviewing:

> (1) experience and behavior questions that elicit *what respondents do or have done*, (2) opinion and value questions that elicit *how respondents think* about their behaviors and experiences, (3) feeling questions that elicit *how respondents react emotionally to or feel about* their experiences and opinions, (4) knowledge questions that elicit *what respondents know* about their worlds, (5) sensory questions that elicit respondents' descriptions of *what and how they see, hear, touch, taste, and smell* in the world around them, and (6) background and demographic questions that elicit *respondents' descriptions of themselves*.
>
> (As reported in LeCompte & Preissle, 2003, p. 171)

We are not endorsing this typology as an exhaustive or even necessarily appropriate list for your topic of interest; we are, though, suggesting that it is helpful to think explicitly about the logic of the types of questions you include.

Interviewing is a skill like any other, and it tends to improve over time. Regarding interviewing skills, Seidman (2013) helpfully suggested that researchers should:

> Listen more, talk less .... Follow up on what the participant says.... Ask questions when you do not understand.... Ask to hear more about a subject.... Explore, don't probe.... Avoid leading questions.... Avoid yes/no questions.... Follow-up, don't interrupt.... Ask participants to tell a story.... Ask for concrete details when you need them.... Follow your hunches.
>
> (pp. 66–75)

Other authors, like Bryman (2006), have suggested a range of types of interview questions. These excellent overviews of interviewing skills can help a researcher become more aware of interaction patterns in interviews, which we believe is critically important for the CCS approach that is premised on the belief that knowledge is not out there to be discovered by the researcher but is socially produced through meaningful interaction.

There are, of course, good reasons *not* to interview. Perhaps an interview will not produce data to answer your research questions. Interviews are good for questions that do not lend themselves to observable moments, such as tracking parents' school choice decisions, but not for questions that are primarily about practices or behaviors. Many qualitative researchers are skeptical about what people say they do and prefer to observe what people actually do, or at least confirm by using interviews and observations (Wolcott, 2008). Further, some intellectual traditions do not consider interview data trustworthy because it is interactionally produced and people accommodate, socially, to what they think the interviewer wants to hear (McDermott & Tylbor, 1983).

In terms of interviewing as a primary method in a comparative case study, there are a few questions you want to ask yourself as you are designing your study. These include the following: How will you present yourself to different groups of interviewees? What obstacles can you anticipate in conducting interviews with different kinds of people and how will you try to prevent those difficulties (Briggs, 1986)? How do you think that data from interviews becomes knowledge (Silverman, 2011)? How do you anticipate analyzing the data produced through interviews (Silverman, 2003, 2011; Wolcott, 2008; Green, Franquiz, & Dixon, 1997; Tilley, 2003)? These and more questions deserve attention if you intend to use interviewing as a research method.

Exercise 3.1 How Might You Use Interviews in a Comparative Case Study?

Interviews are a fundamental method for qualitative researchers. As you consider the use of interviews in your comparative case study, ask yourself these questions:

- What categories or groups of people might I interview? List them in your fieldnotes.
- What format of interview might I use with each group listed above—structured, semi-structured, or unstructured—and why?
- What themes would I include in the interview guide for each group listed above? Make a brief list for each guide and add this to your fieldnotes.
- What is my plan for piloting each interview guide before using it?

Observations

The other qualitative research method that is often used in comparative case studies, especially to develop the horizontal axis, is observation. Much has been written about observation, and we do not wish to repeat it here (e.g., Agar, 1980; Atkinson & Hammersley, 1994; Babbie, 2015; DeWalt & DeWalt, 2011; LeCompte & Priessle, 2003; Lofland & Lofland, 1994; Whyte, 1984). Instead, our purpose is to highlight aspects of observing with particular relevance for a CCS researcher. Like interviews, observation techniques range from full observer (not interacting with participants, only observing) to participant observation (engaging in a more or less limited way with participants) to full participant (Adler & Adler, 1994). While positivist researchers are very concerned about the impact of the observer on the behavior of those being observed, many social scientists counter that their long engagement with a particular group of participants increases the validity of observation data, including participant observation data (Maxwell, 2013). Besides, as Hammersley and Atkinson argue, "In a sense, all social research is a form of participant observation, because we cannot study the social world without being a part of it" (1983, p. 249).

Observation entails spending long periods of time watching people. It may be structured by using an observation tool, such as a checklist or tally sheet upon which certain behaviors, words, or activities are recorded at intervals during an observation period. These tools can facilitate comparison across sites and with multiple researchers. For example, our work with Tanzanian and U.S. researchers in classrooms across six Tanzanian secondary schools used an observation tool in which each researcher recorded how the teacher started the lesson, used the chalkboard, and asked questions of students, among other items. The researchers found it easiest to take unstructured but copious notes during the lesson and then later answer structured questions about the way the lesson began, how the board was utilized, and so forth. However, they did keep a tally sheet of the kinds of questions asked by the teacher, contrasting closed questions with a correct answer and more open questions that allowed students to interpret or analyze. The Tanzanian and U.S. researchers observing the same lesson could then compare their answers, and the research team could compare across the 23 teachers in the six schools in the study (Vavrus & Bartlett, 2013).

Participant observation and full participation entail spending equally long, if not longer, periods of time interacting with people than when one is solely an observer. Participating involves asking people about what you are seeing them do and hearing them say, and it is often less structured because these questions tend to arise while the researcher is participating alongside those in the study. For example, Lesley Bartlett used a range of observation techniques when she conducted research in Brazil on youth and adult literacy programs that use Freirean pedagogy. She observed teacher training events; she was a participant observer in seven literacy classrooms; and she lived in the community with the students and teachers, conducting participant observation in community stores, at work with participants, and in homes to get a sense of how they used and talked about reading and writing in classrooms and beyond (Bartlett, 2009). This example illustrates the importance of "thinking carefully about what is being seen, interpreting it, and talking to the actors to check the emerging interpretations" (Delamont, 2007, p. 206). Both participant observation and full participation entail informal interviewing in the course of research, and one may select different levels of engagement for different research questions or for different phases of the study.

Like other elements of a comparative case study, observations deserve (but often do not receive) careful attention to questions of sampling. Ask yourself who or what you will observe, where, when, how, and why. Be clear about these answers; write them down in your fieldnotes. Revisit them over the course of the study because your strategies may change as new hunches develop from the fieldwork. One research question may require one observation strategy, while another may require a different strategy or no observations at all. For example, a project interested in why youth use drugs could involve mostly interviews; a question on how and when students talk about drugs requires observations at carefully selected sites.

We have found that CCS researchers find it helpful to maximally diversify what and who they observe in the early phases of the study. This is important because it helps in making decisions about what constitutes the case itself and what sites might be important for further research. Later in the study, the researcher can engage in more focused observations in fewer sites. We find that it is also important to ask ourselves a series of reflexive questions about our role in the activity being observed, such as how fully we should be engaged, how our engagement might influence the participants, how well some participants (but not others) know us, and how much some participants know about our research. Remember that participant observation is a fundamentally experiential, embodied, and interactional approach to research. Your engagement with others may be shaped by their reading of your ethnicity, gender, class, speech, education, religion, and other identity markers just as you may observe and interpret their actions differently based on these markers.

Observing, like interviewing, is a skill that should improve over time, with practice and with careful reading of available methods literature. It helps to practice during a pilot study or on a different project before engaging in your major research. Before every observation, it is critical to develop a plan for *how* you are going to look. What are you looking for? Will you use any tools to train your gaze? Why or why not? How will you record your data during observations? Remember that observations are meant to be descriptive, and there is little time for analysis when one is trying to jot down what is occurring during a meeting, class, or political rally. Thus, we encourage you to make jottings or notes (most often in a notebook) that are as detailed as is feasible in the situation and to note 'time stamps' in the margins periodically (e.g., every 5-10 minutes).

After the observation, be sure you leave sufficient time for elaborating on your fieldnotes. This is a crucial step where you turn the short notes or jottings into detailed accounts of what you observed. It is best done while the details are fresh in your mind, preferably the same day. In addition, we suggest that you leave time to reflect on the observation experience itself. What were the most important things you learned? What went well? What did not, and how could you change it in the future? What did you miss? What should be your next step, methodologically, given what you learned? Good observers are systematic about observing, recording what they observing, reflecting on those observations, and storing their observations in an easily accessible system.

In some familiar settings like schools and medical clinics, the greatest challenges may be overfamiliarity and boredom. Delamont (2012) emphasized the importance of focusing on "what is happening rather than what one 'expects,' 'knows' and is familiar with" (p. 345). She also insisted that the observer must avoid judgment. She wrote, "The researcher's job is to find out what the participants think is going on, what they do, why they do it, how they do it and what is 'normal' and 'odd' for them" (p. 346). Seeing things afresh, or what some call "strange-making," is particularly important for horizontal comparisons because the sites may start to lose their 'strangeness' and uniqueness when we focus on the common elements in an observation guide.

Exercise 3.2 How Might You Use Observations in a Comparative Case Study?

Observations are another essential method for comparative case studies. Make a table in your fieldnotes where you consider the following questions:

- What are essential events for me to observe, and why?
- How frequently do I want to observe these events, and for how long a period of time?
- Will I be a full observer, a participant observer, or a full participant during each category of events, and why?
- During each category of observations, what specifically will I be looking for? Do I need an observation guide or tool of any sort for any of these observations?
- What is my plan for writing fieldnotes during and after each observation?

Expect to update this table as the study develops.

Interviewing and observation are essential tools in social research generally and in most comparative case studies. Below, we show how these methods have been used effectively to develop the horizontal axis of the two different kinds of comparative case studies.

Horizontal Comparisons Using Homologous Units

Homologous comparative case studies select homologous units of analysis for comparison. For example, a project might contrast the 'discrepant and idiosyncratic' implementation of the U.S. federal No Child Left Behind policy across states (e.g., Davidson, Reback, Rockoff, & Schwartz, 2015), or it might juxtapose hidden curricula in socioeconomically dissimilar schools in one state (e.g., Anyon 1980). The examples below demonstrate the value of sound homologous comparison of units that share some corresponding features—they are all in the category of 'state' or 'family' or 'school,' for instance. In some of the examples, the researcher limits herself primarily to horizontal comparison; in later examples, the scholar engages in vertical or transversal comparison as well, which we recommend. However, our aim in this section is to best illustrate homologous horizontal comparison.

Example 3.1: *Annette Lareau's* Unequal Childhoods

Annette Lareau's rightly famous book, *Unequal Childhoods*, provides an excellent example of how to integrate observations and interviews, and how to use homologous cases for horizontal comparison (2011). Lareau was interested in how parenting and childhood in the U.S. vary by social class. To pursue this topic, she selected twelve families, each of which had a child who was nine or ten years old at the time. She stratified the sample by sex (half girls, half boys) and class, seeking equal representation among families designated middle class, working class, and poor. She also sought to include white and African American families across each sample (see her methodological appendix). Lareau hired a team of fieldworkers; together, they observed each family and focal child approximately twenty times during a one month period in order to gain insights into daily life and family dynamics across settings, including school functions, extracurricular events, church, etc. They paid particular attention to the organization of daily life, language use, and interactions with major institutions. As background to the study, Lareau also used observations across two schools and in-depth interviews with 88 families. In sum, Lareau found that middle-class parents engaged in "concerned cultivation," wherein they constantly fostered and assessed their children's various talents (e.g., through extracurricular lessons and experiences). They also intervened on their children's behalf with teachers, coaches, and other leaders; they instilled a sense of entitlement in their children; and they taught the children how to advocate for themselves and how important social institutions worked. The study showed very clearly how resource- and time-intensive this parenting strategy is. In contrast, among the working-class and poor families, Lareau documented a strategy she dubbed "natural accomplishment of growth," a less-structured strategy focused on providing for children's basic needs while allowing talents to develop organically. In these families, children have fewer structured activities and clearer boundaries between adults and children. While Lareau pointed out the advantages of this strategy, including more autonomy and more respectful (and less entitled) children, she ultimately concluded that major institutions (especially schools) unevenly reward middle-class versions of childhood.

There are a variety of conceptual and methodological critiques of Lareau's book, and they merit consideration. Here, though, our purpose is to highlight the elements of the study that produced a commendable and highly influential homologous comparison. First, Lareau developed a careful conceptual frame, based on Bourdieu's notion of cultural capital; this frame informed her study design such that she focused on families—the homologous units—that differed by race and social class. Second, Lareau conducted a preliminary phase of research, which entailed interviews with the parents of 31 third-grade children from one elementary school. We, too, advocate for phased research because better selection decisions can often be made after the first phase of a project. In Lareau's case, this preliminary phase led her to include race as a criterion and to broaden her definition of social class to include the kind of jobs parents had and their level of education. Her realization during this early phase that a "substantial number of children were from households supported by public assistance" led her to add a group of poor families "not involved in the labor market" (p. 347). Third, Lareau added another phase of observations at two racially integrated schools. These experiences helped Lareau specify the research questions— whether class or race most influenced parenting strategies, institutional engagement, and academic success—which she used to inform her sampling strategy for the third phase of the study that included in-depth observations and interviews in twelve households. Lareau skillfully wove into her study unstructured observations, structured observations, unstructured interviews, and structured interviews, varying her methods across the period of data collection to meet specific purposes.

Lareau's study is remarkable for its depth and breadth, given how labor-intensive interviewing and observing can be. She did, though, have the advantage of a funded project, a research team, and years of research experience when she embarked on the *Unequal Childhoods* study. However, many doctoral students and early-career faculty do individual projects that employ a homologous case selection logic with similarly successful results. Below, we consider two such cases.

Example 3.2: Bethany Wilinski's Study of Early Childhood Education in Wisconsin

Bethany Wilinski (2014, forthcoming) employed what we would call a comparative case study with a homologous horizontal axis to understand the rapid expansion of publicly funded pre-kindergarten (pre-K, or what Wisconsin has called 4K) programs, which promise to close the achievement gap and redress economic and racial inequalities. Her work focused on three teachers in three different institutions in one Wisconsin city (which she dubbed Lakeville) and how they were influenced by district, state, and federal policy shifts. Wilinski asked: "How do 4K teachers understand, appropriate, and enact Lakeville's 4K policy? What forces affect teachers' appropriation and enactment of the policy?" To pursue these questions, Wilinski conducted research over a period of one year with three pre-K teachers located in three different institutions—a public school, a private non-profit preschool, and a private for-profit corporate childcare center— because she wanted to see how 4K in Lakeville is enacted in a range of public and private sites. This selection of different types of pre-kindergarten schools with different fee structures implied diverse student populations in the study as well. This case selection was critical to her ability to generate insights regarding how institutional settings and student populations, combined with teachers' pedagogical understandings, training, and career goals, shaped policy appropriation.

Wilinski examined how these teachers understood and enacted the 4K policy, and what the policy came to mean to them and their institution. She found that the district policy had created a new cadre of pre-K teachers with similar qualifications but who enacted policy under dramatically different working conditions and compensation schemes. This, then, reshaped relationships and hierarchies within and across institutions and made inequalities between early childhood education teachers and public school teachers increasingly visible and relevant. The policy influenced teachers' job satisfaction, school district-community site relations, and the structure of early childhood education in Lakeville, with serious implications for the status of teachers, families' access to programs, and children's early education experiences.

The homologous horizontal axis of Wilinski's study combined with the vertical axis because she also analyzed Lakeville's 4K policy in relation to pre-K policy at the state and national levels. This vertical element of the analysis provides a way to understand how a school district and individual schools are situated within a broader set of political, social, and economic relations that structure how 4K policy is conceptualized and implemented. Further, through horizontal comparison of three teachers' work in one district (another example of a homologous comparison in her study), Wilinski demonstrated how a particular 4K policy aimed at equalizing early learning opportunities for young children simultaneously created and perpetuated hierarchies and inequalities that affected individuals and institutions. Wilinski's dissertation exemplifies how doctoral students can successfully blend horizontal and vertical axes.

An informed site selection strategy was crucial to the success of Wilinski's comparative case study. It did not occur by chance. She conducted a pilot study of 4K programs in two private and two public sites the year before she began her doctoral research. As a result of that experience, she realized that she needed to include different *types* of private sites. This led her to add the for-profit corporate site. Wilinski also realized that she needed to frame her sample in terms of institutional type and not student population because childcare sites do not only serve their immediate surrounding community. Wilinski reported that the pacing of her time in the sites changed as she negotiated access. She initially wanted to do fieldwork in all three sites concurrently because she thought that the rhythm of the school year might be important. However, the conditions of access forced her to stagger her entry into the sites, which allowed her to have several weeks to a month of intensive fieldwork in each site for the first phase of research. In the second phase, she spent equal amounts of time in each site, and the total number of observation hours per site was ultimately quite equal. This unplanned observation strategy allowed Wilinski to observe each site on its own terms, rather than forcing her into a comparative frame from the beginning. Finally, as the fieldwork unfolded, she realized that it would be important to attend as many district-wide meetings as possible because these events offered critical perspectives on the experiences of individual teachers in their specific schools; they allowed Wilinski to understand both individual teachers and their specific institutions as part of the larger 4K system in Lakeville.

Example 3.3: Michelle Bellino's Study of Civic Education in Guatemala

Michelle Bellino (2014, 2015, 2016) conducted a comparative case study to consider civic education in 'post-war' Guatemala, a country beleaguered by chronic violence in the aftermath of a 36-year civil war. She asked how adolescents "draw on their construction of the violent past to shape their sense of civic identity" (2014, p. 85). From 2010 to 2012, she conducted fourteen months of fieldwork for her dissertation in Guatemala City and the rural province of Izabal; her fieldwork entailed participant observation in four schools—two urban and two rural. Each school had different experiences with violence, past and present. As Bellino noted, "the comparative sites not only serve as divergent and oppositional cases, but also as relational compositions situated within a whole" (p. 91). Bellino spent at least four weeks in each community, attending classes, visiting homes, attending community and youth group meetings, public commemorations, and religious events, and participating in formal and informal activities throughout the day. In schools, she observed broadly, but focused particularly on social studies classrooms. In addition to intensive observations, she conducted interviews with teachers, parents, and students to explore how youth make meaning of their educational encounters with injustice, and particularly how they understand the role and relevance of the war in their 'postwar' lives.

In an article based on her dissertation (2016), Bellino engaged a CCS approach to analyze a globally-influenced but state-led curricular reform in Guatemala. She showed "how state actors envisioned narrating the postwar transition for both national citizens and the global world" (p. 63). She also drew upon observational data to describe "the varied ways in which young people [were] presented with knowledge and attitudes about historical injustice in formal education," and she analyzed "the ways that young people [were] positioned as civic actors in the 'postwar' era" (p. 60). To do so, Bellino used horizontal comparison to juxtapose teaching and learning in one urban and one rural classroom, showing how different teachers adopted, challenged, or rejected these reforms, and "examining how particular depictions of war are positioned as civic narratives for different identity groups, set against the backdrop of particular ways of understanding the 'postwar'" (p. 60). Her comparison demonstrated how legacies of war have been exacerbated through an unequal educational system. Further, engaging a historical perspective (and what we would call the transversal axis), her horizontal comparison showed how local histories and experiences with the state during the war differentially affected civic engagement.

Overall, in Bellino's work, horizontal comparisons among the four schools illustrated how a history of conflict and a national curricular reform were radically reinterpreted and enacted across different sites.

Exercise 3.3 How Might You Design a Homologous Horizontal Comparison?

Bethany Wilinski examined how three teachers in three very different institutional contexts implemented a city pre-K educational policy, which was itself influenced by state and federal pre-K policies. Michelle Bellino conducted fieldwork in two urban and two rural schools in Guatemala to explore how students interpreted their civic efficacy and opportunities for civic engagement in light of past and on-going violence, and how teachers implemented civic education.

As you reflect on these horizontal comparisons, ask yourself:

- Are there relevant policies, programs, curricula, or historical trends that have influenced the phenomenon that interests you in your own research project?
- How might your project engage a homologous horizontal comparison? What sampling logic would you employ, and why?
- If you were to use homologous horizontal comparison in one phase of your research, would you choose to do it early in the project, to generate a sense of how similar phenomena play out in different contexts, or late in the project, to re-consider propositions that emerged from your single case study? Why?
- Might you choose to "nest" homologous comparisons? If so, what would the sites or cases be?
- How might your research questions shift if you engage homologous horizontal comparison at some stage of the project?

Horizontal Comparisons Using Heterologous Units

Heterologous horizontal comparison is generally guided by a logic of connection; though juxtaposition is possible, usually this type of work seeks to *trace* a phenomenon across sites at the same relative scale. Heterologous comparison features in many multi-sited ethnographies because researchers are tracing a phenomenon across different sites and spaces at the same scale, such as Desmond's (2016) study of eviction in Milwaukee mentioned above and Karen Ho's (2009) examination of Wall Street's investment banks that involved interviews and observations across institutions, out-placement agencies, conferences, and social venues. In many cases, the heterologous comparison at one scale is nested in a homologous comparison at another, as in the Kendall and Bajaj studies discussed below that compared across states in the U.S. and India, respectively, but then examined heterologous sites within them.

Example 3.4: Nancy Kendall's Sex Education Debates

Nancy Kendall's research (2008, 2012) considers the shifting role of the U.S. federal government in sex education. Given the highly decentralized nature of schooling in the U.S., the federal government played no significant role in directing state policies or local sexuality education programs until 1996, when then-president Bill Clinton signed a congressional bill that set aside almost half a billion dollars for "abstinence only until marriage" (AOUM) education. Federal AOUM funding expanded further under President George Bush, and the definitions of AOUM programs became more precise. When states began to reject the conditions of federal AOUM funds, the federal government responded by bypassing the states and channeling federal funds directly to nongovernmental (often faith-based) organizations. Kendall noted that these funding shifts strengthened NGOs' capacity to provide free AOUM education for schools at the same time that state and federal high-stakes accountability measures (such as No Child Left Behind) placed increased academic (and assessment) demands on schools, diluting their attention for sex education.

Kendall (2012) considered these historical shifts at the federal level, and she then used observations and interviews to conduct comparative, multi-sited research on sex education policy as practice in five states: California, Florida, Maryland, Wisconsin, and Wyoming. This focus on similar units of analysis (e.g., states) illustrates homologous case selection. She purposefully selected states that differed in their sex education policies— from providing no guidance to adopting varieties of either AOUME or comprehensive sex education.

Kendall not only compared state policy related to sex education; she also examined a number of heterologous sites in different communities. In each state, examining sex education policy and practice led her to trace crucial strands of local and state politics and socio-economic relations that were influencing how sex education was framed in school districts and local schools. For example, through fieldwork at schools, school board meetings, and community groups in Wyoming, Kendall (2012) showed how libertarianism and the politics of White and Native American relations influenced local sex education debates and practices. In comparison, in California, the focal school's sex education practices were largely shaped by state policy, the school's own tracking system, and the availability of a non-profit comprehensive sex education provider in the area. Fieldwork in California entailed interviewing about and observing the non-profit's sex education programming as it was taught in the different tracked classrooms, observing how school leaders discussed and negotiated state policy, talking to state officials about how they constructed state sex education policy, and visiting with community members who were trying to organize to change state policy.

Kendall's study of homologous and heterologous horizontal sites was embedded in and organized by a vertical comparison in which she examined district, state, and national sites, and by the development of a transversal axis that illuminated shifts over time in U.S. federal sex education policy. The vertical comparison provided a cross-state, comparative framework that shaped the focus and comparative lens adopted in the interviews and observations that she conducted at schools, in community organizations, in district offices, and in state and national governmental and nongovernmental organizations across the country. However, she sought, primarily, to understand the contemporary context in which federal funding "interacted with state, district, school, and classroom practices to shape students' experiences with sexuality in schools" (2012, p. 15).

Thus, Kendall's work incorporated multiple types and axes of comparison to produce a rich, complex study of sex education policy. She argued, and we concur, that using such a comparative approach "challenges policy literatures that assume a unilinear impact model," and allows for more dynamic research on sex education, in this case, that moves from the "study of a bounded geographic site … to an idea of place as 'always formed through relations and connections with dynamics at play in other places, and in wider regional, national, and transnational arenas'" (2012, pp. 14–16). In this way, Kendall's work exemplifies the best of the CCS approach.

Example 3.5: Monisha Bajaj's Study of Human Rights Education in India

In her study of human rights education (HRE) in India, Monisha Bajaj (2012) made judicious use of heterologous horizontal comparisons. Bajaj focused on a very influential national NGO, the Institute of Human Rights Education (part of the larger human rights NGO People's Watch), which was active in 18 states across India. Engaging a historical perspective, her study presented the key events that led to the growth and expansion of the Institute's programs. To better understand this national-scale organization, she employed observations at IHRE-sponsored teacher trainings in multiple states, a national HRE conference, and National Advisory Committee meetings in New Delhi, among other activities. She demonstrated how, over time, the Institute gained support for HRE in a crowded curricular field by engaging in what she called "persuasive pragmatism" (p. 54).

To map the contemporary landscape of HRE, Bajaj decided to focus on six states. She narrowed her selection of states to include those states that had completed at least one three-year cycle of the HRE program and had alumni from the program that could be interviewed; she also sought regional diversity in the sample of states. With 13 months of fieldwork conducted from 2008 to 2010, she carried out surveys (completed with a team of assistants) in hundreds of schools in the six focal states.[2] State visits varied in duration from ten days to two months, depending on issues of sampling and the scope of the program(s) in operation. Bajaj sought to spend enough time in each site to understand the challenges facing HRE programs as well as the successes they may have achieved. Bajaj paired this breadth with the depth of information provided by conducting focus groups, interviews, and observations at more than 60 schools and with

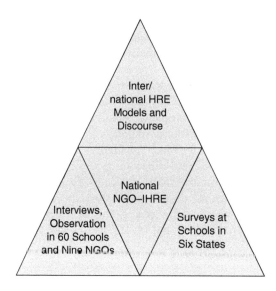

Figure 3.1 Monisha Bajaj's Comparative Case Study of Human Rights Education in India.

nine different NGOs (most affiliated with the IHRE). She was particularly attentive to how teachers and students interpreted and took up HRE. Throughout the project, Bajaj employed maximum variation sampling to include a variety of schools in distinct parts of the states visited (urban and rural), and a diversity of respondents based on religion, caste, age, length of time learning/teaching HRE, gender, and educational background. Respondents included 118 HRE teachers, 625 students, 80 staff, and policymakers of HRE (see Figure 3.1).

Bajaj paired this school-level focus with attention to the vertical and transversal axes as well. She used secondary literature and interviews to chart the rise of HRE in India over the past three decades in policy discussions and in NGO models. She examined the work done by heterologous governmental bodies at the national scale—specifically, the National Council of Educational Research and Training (NCERT), the National Council for Teacher Education (NCTE), the University Grants Commission (UGC), and the National Human Rights Commission (NHRC)—to incorporate HRE into their work. She also analyzed national policy documents, such as National Curriculum Frameworks that influence and guide educational planning and practice as well as teacher formation nationwide. During her school-based fieldwork, Bajaj was then able to consider how national curricula and policies were taken up, contested, or ignored (2012).

Thus, Bajaj (2012) exemplifies how to integrate heterologous and homologous horizontal comparison, vertical comparison, and transversal comparison in a single project to illuminate a central phenomenon of interest—HRE in India. Her work also offers an extended rumination on the question of how to use schooling to redress various forms of inequality.

Exercise 3.4 How Might You Design a Heterologous Horizontal Comparison?

In her comparative study of sexual education in the United States, Nancy Kendall included heterologous sites—classrooms, schools, and NGOs—across five states. Examining human rights education, Monisha Bajaj conducted observations, interviews, and focus group discussions in schools and NGOs across six states. As you reflect on these multi-sited versions of heterologous horizontal comparison, both of which also integrated other varieties of comparison, ask yourself:

- Are you more comfortable with homologous or heterologous comparisons? Why? Which might be more appropriate for the problem under consideration in your research?
- Given your topic, what sites do you initially expect you would include in a homologous and/or heterologous horizontal comparison? Why?
- What sites would you not include? Why?
- If you were to engage a multi-sited study, how would you make and adequately document emergent decisions about sites to include in your study?

Conclusion

In this chapter, we described the first of the three axes in a comparative case study: the horizontal axis. We distinguished between a homologous horizontal comparison, which includes corresponding units of analysis, and a heterologous horizontal comparison, which selects sites of different types that are more or less at the same scale. We noted that horizontal comparisons are often nested or embedded in comparison at another scale, such as when a study looks at four human rights NGOs in the capital cities in two different states. Such studies invoke the vertical axis as they trace across scales while simultaneously comparing at the same scale. We also gave a brief overview of two research methods—interviewing and observations—that are often used in developing the horizontal axis (as well as the vertical and transversal as we will see in later chapters) before discussing five exemplary horizontal comparisons.

As we have shown, some studies will use only horizontal comparisons. However, the type of work we promote incorporates vertical and/or transversal perspectives as well. We turn now to consider the vertical axis in greater depth.

Notes

1 For more on embedded case studies, see Scholz and Tietje (2002).
2 We discuss surveying as a method in Chapter 5.

References

Adler, P. A., & Adler, P. (1994). Observational techniques. In N. Denzin & Y. Lincoln, (Eds.), *Handbook of qualitative research* (pp. 377–392). Thousand Oaks, CA: Sage.

Agar, M. (1980). *The professional stranger.* San Diego: Academic Press.

Anyon, J. (1980). Social class and the hidden curriculum of work. *Journal of Education 162*, 67–92.

Atkinson, P., & Hammersley, M. (1994). Ethnography and participant observation. In N. Denzin and Y. Lincoln, (Eds.), *Handbook of qualitative inquiry* (pp. 248–261). Thousand Oaks, CA: Sage.

Babbie, E. (2015). *Observing ourselves: Essays in social research* (2nd ed.). Long Grove, IL: Waveland Press.

Bajaj, M. (2012). *Schooling for social change: The rise and impact of human rights education in India.* New York: Bloomsbury Academic.

Bartlett, L. (2009). *The word and the world: The cultural politics of literacy in Brazil.* New York: Hampton Press.

Bellino, M. J. (2014). *Memory in transition: Historical consciousness and civic attitudes among youth in "postwar" Guatemala* (unpublished doctoral dissertation). Harvard University, Cambridge, MA.

Bellino, M. J. (2015). The risks we are willing to take: Youth civic development in "postwar" Guatemala. *Harvard Educational Review 85*(4), 537–561.

Bellino, M. J. (2016). So that we do not fall again: History education and citizenship in "postwar" Guatemala. *Comparative Education Review 60*(1), 58–79.

Briggs, C. (1986). *Learning how to ask: A sociolinguistic appraisal of the role of the interview in social science research.* Cambridge: Cambridge University Press.

Bryman, A. (2006). *Social research methods.* New York: Oxford University Press.

Davidson, E., Reback, R., Rockoff, J., & Schwartz, H. (2015). Fifty ways to leave a child behind: Idiosyncrasies and discrepancies in states' implementation of NCLB. *Educational Researcher 44*(6), 347–358.

Delamont, S. (2007). Ethnography and participant observation. In C. Seale, G. Goto, J. F. Gubrium, & D. Silverman (Eds.), *Qualitative research practice* (pp. 205–217). Thousand Oaks, CA: Sage.

Delamont, S. (Ed.) (2012). *The handbook of qualitative research in education.* Northampton, MA: Edward Elgar Publishing.

Desmond, M. (2016). *Evicted: Poverty and profit in the American city.* New York: Crown.

DeWalt, K., & DeWalt, B. (2011). *Participant observation: A guide for fieldworkers* (2nd ed.). Lanham, MD: Altamira Press.

Falzon, M. (2009). *Multi-sited ethnography: Theory, praxis, and locality in contemporary research.* New York: Routledge.

Ferguson, J. (2012). Novelty and method: Reflections on global fieldwork. In S. Coleman & P. von Hellermann (Eds.), *Multi-sited ethnography: Problems and possibilities in the translocation of research methods* (pp. 194–208). New York: Routledge.

Green, J., Franquiz, M., & Dixon, C. (1997). The myth of the objective transcript. *TESOL Quarterly 31*(1), 172–176.

Hammersley, M., & P. Atkinson (1983). *Ethnography: Principles in practice*. London: Tavistock.

Heyl, B. S. (2001). Ethnographic interviewing. In P. Atkinson, A. Coffey, S. Delamont, J. Lofland, & L. Lofland (Eds.), *Handbook of ethnography* (pp. 248–261). London: Sage.

Ho, K. (2009). *Liquidated: An ethnography of Wall Street*. Durham, NC: Duke University Press.

Kendall, N. (2008). Sexuality education in an abstinence-only era: A comparative case study of two U.S. states. *Sexuality Research and Social Policy* 5(2), 23–44.

Kendall, N. (2012). *The sex education debates*. Chicago: University of Chicago Press.

Kvale, S. (1996). *InterViews: An introduction to qualitative research interviewing*. Thousand Oaks, CA: Sage.

Lareau, A. (2011). *Unequal childhoods: Class, race, and family life* (2nd ed.). Berkeley: University of California Press.

LeCompte, M., & Preissle, J. (2003). *Ethnography and qualitative design in educational research* (2nd ed.). New York: Academic Press.

LeCompte, M., & Schensul, J. (2010). *Designing and conducting ethnographic research*. Lanham, MD: Altamira.

Lofland, J., & Lofland, L. (1994). *Analyzing social settings: A guide to qualitative observation and analysis*. Belmont, CA: Wadsworth Publishing.

Maxwell, J. (2013). *Qualitative research design: An interactive approach*. Thousand Oaks, CA: Sage.

May, T. (2001). *Social research: Issues, methods, and process* (3rd ed.). Maidenhead, UK: Open University Press.

McDermott, R., & Tylbor, H. (1983). On the necessity of collusion in conversation. *Text* 3(3), 277–297.

O'Reilly, K. (2005). *Ethnographic methods*. London: Routledge.

O'Reilly, K. (2009). *Key concepts in ethnography*. Thousand Oaks, CA: Sage.

Patton, M. (2001). *Qualitative research and evaluation methods*. Thousand Oaks, CA: Sage.

Pope, D. (2001). *Doing school: How we are creating a generation of stressed out, materialistic, and miseducated students*. New Haven, CT: Yale.

Reichman, D. (2011). *The broken village: Coffee, migration, and globalization in Honduras*. Ithaca, NY: Cornell University Press.

Roy, A. (2010). *Poverty capital: Microfinance and the making of development*. New York: Routledge.

Rubin, H. J., & Rubin, I. S. (1995). *Qualitative interviewing: The art of hearing data*. London: Sage.

Scholz, R., & Tietje, O. (2002). *Embedded case study methods*. Thousand Oaks, CA: Sage.

Seidman, I. E. (2013). *Interviewing as qualitative research* (4th ed.). New York: Teachers College Press.

Silverman, D. (2003). Analyzing talk and text. In N. Denzin & Y. Lincoln (Eds.), *Collecting and interpreting qualitative materials* (pp. 340–362). Thousand Oaks, CA: Sage.

Silverman, D. (2011). *Interpreting qualitative data* (4th ed.). Thousand Oaks, CA: Sage.

Tilley, S. (2003). "Challenging" research practices: Turning a critical lens on the work of transcription. *Qualitative Inquiry* 9(5), 750–773.

van der Veer, P. (2013). *The value of comparison.* Transcript of the Lewis Henry Morgan Lecture given on November 13, 2013. Available at http://www.haujournal.org/vanderVeer_TheValueOfComparison_LHML_Transcript.pdf.

van der Veer, P. (2016). *The value of comparison.* Durham, NC: Duke University Press.

Vavrus, F., & Bartlett, L. (2013). *Teaching in tension: International pedagogies, national policies, and teachers' practices in Tanzania.* Rotterdam: Sense Publishers.

Whyte, W. F. (1984). *Learning from the field.* Thousand Oaks, CA: Sage.

Wilinski, B. (2014). *"I don't want preK to turn into school": What preK policy means in practice* (unpublished doctoral dissertation). University of Wisconsin, Madison.

Wilinski, B. (forthcoming). *When preK comes to school.* New York: Teachers College Press.

Wolcott, H. (2008). *Ethnography: A way of seeing.* Lanham, MD: Altamira Press.

4   Vertical Comparison

The use of the term *vertical* in the CCS approach opens up analytical opportunities but also risks conceptual constriction if one sees it as a study of levels rather than of networks. If we picture for a moment a high-rise office building that houses the staff of a company, one could conduct a study that compares the way that lower-level workers on the first few floors and senior management on the upper floors interpret and enact the company's mission on corporate social responsibility. Such a study would literally be a vertical comparison and might generate insights into how gender, class, race, and age influence the interpretation of social responsibility. However, an interpretation of the vertical axis as a comparison of pre-determined stratified levels (e.g., the administrative staff on the second floor; the regional managers on the twelfth) does not allow for the study of interactions among the employees with different positions in the company or for informal flows of knowledge from one floor in the building to another that one cannot necessarily anticipate before launching a research project.

If we were, instead, to trace the process by which the company's mission statement came into being through a complex network of people on many different floors in this building and at the company's offices in other states or countries, we would have a very different, and more dynamic, study. We would be acknowledging that social relations are complex and extend beyond the confines of any pre-defined grouping or level; that alliances and factions within a network are not stable but neither are they random or divorced from broader relations of power; and that authoritative texts like mission statements and national policy draw on knowledge from multiple sources that circulate globally.

Policy sociologist Stephen Ball (2016) recently proposed that scholars of policy focus more on policy networks and policy mobility, by which he means the ways that policy travels through assemblages of actors in bits and pieces rather than as coherent packages. To understand this movement, Ball argued that this means attending to multiple sites, spaces, and scales of policy within and between states and the interactions, relations and movements between them; both national and local unevenness and frictions; urban/rural differences; and different speeds of change and moments of possibility in different localities.

(p. 2)

He called for network analysis and network ethnography, or ethnographies of policy networks, in ways that are similar to the cases we discuss in this chapter, but we elaborate on methods that help delineate the vertical and horizontal axes of a comparative case study.

In the previous chapter, we considered how one can trace processes horizontally as they unfold across homologous sites, such as multiple companies or NGOs working on the same issue in a similar physical space or social arena. One could, for example, compare how corporate social responsibility is defined and operationalized in the mission statements of several similar sized companies based in an urban area where voters have demanded evidence of such responsible actions. In this chapter, we add a vertical axis to the horizontal in examining studies that have explored a phenomenon across homologous sites *and* have traced connections among actors and authoritative texts at different scales. For example, Meg Gardinier (2012, 2014) examined the role of key educational actors in Albanian educational reform and democratization following the fall of the communist dictatorship. In the post-communist period, Albanian policymakers increasingly adopted internationally prevalent models of education for a democratic, market-based, global knowledge society. Yet, despite a seeming convergence of national and international educational aims, such interventions resulted in a wide variation of results on the ground. Based on 32 months of multi-sited ethnographic fieldwork, Gardinier investigated the changing roles and identities, sources of knowledge, and professional practice of international experts, national education leaders, and teachers as they developed and implemented educational projects for democratic citizenship and the global knowledge economy. She found that, although national policymakers aimed to modernize the Albanian education system by infusing international models, teachers strategically interpreted and adapted these foreign models to reflect their experience with the political context of schools, their pedagogical and subject knowledge, and their familiar forms of teaching practice. The vertical axis reminds us to follow the phenomenon itself, be it a practice or a policy, as it enlists and engages actors whom one might otherwise assume operate in bounded spaces.

The examples we have selected for this chapter are two particularly rich studies whose vertical dimensions are enhanced through their use of analytical tools that show how people, objects, and discourses are connected through policy. Although the study of policy is not the only purpose for the kind of comparison we put forward in this chapter, it is a particularly appropriate one for reasons laid out in the next section. As we discussed in previous chapters, an approach to policy studies that treats the nation-state as an entity unto itself is woefully inadequate in an era when new forms of global governance affect policymaking in nations both large and small. The same can be said for ethnographic studies of a single site that do not recognize the networks of local and national (and frequently international) human actors and non-human actants that interact and reshape practice in specific cases.

The first study we examine is Jill Koyama's deeply engaging book, *Making Failure Pay: For-Profit Tutoring, High-Stakes Testing, and Public Schools* (2010), which adeptly used actor network theory to develop vertical and horizontal comparisons in its analysis of No Child Left Behind (NCLB), the U.S. education act that went into effect in 2002 and shaped national, state, and district policy for more than a decade. The second example is Christina Kwauk's exemplary dissertation, *Playing for the Future: Sport and the Production of Healthy Bodies in Policy and Practice* (2014), a study that used critical discourse analysis to explore the global sport for development movement and how it is manifested through policies affecting everyday life on the Pacific Island nation of Sāmoa, a country with one of the highest rates of obesity in the world. Although there are many other examples we could have explored in this chapter, the studies by Koyama and Kwauk are particularly important owing to their disavowal of rigid local/national/global levels in their analyses and their embrace of network and discourse analysis.

Vertical Comparison: Central Assumptions

We have already discussed the rationale for vertical comparison, but it is useful to review some of our central assumptions to make clear why this dimension of the CCS approach is particularly relevant for the study of policy. These assumptions are related to the discussion of culture, context, and comparison in Chapter 1, and they can be summarized as follows:

- Comparison of homologous entities at the same scale, such as two primary schools in the same city or four health-care providers in a single county, runs the risk of reifying culture when the actions and discourses of a group of actors are disconnected from the sociopolitical context in which they are situated. The study of policy, however, encourages us to consider how actors respond similarly *and* differently to a mandate from state or federal authorities even though the actors are putatively 'of' the same culture. Their variable appropriation of policy as discourse and as practice is often due to different histories of racial, ethnic, or gender politics in their communities that appropriately complicate the notion of a single cultural group.
- Comparative research often begins by selecting, *a priori*, multiple contexts of different scales for a study, such as an examination of global agricultural policy, comparing its effects on corn farmers in Kansas and on the staff at the Food and Agricultural Organization (FAO) in Rome. Although this may lead to interesting findings, it overdetermines the geographical distinction and physical distance between these two settings without considering the

networks in which they may be mutually enmeshed (Leander & Sheehy, 2004). We assume, instead, that the context in such a study would be established by tracing the formation and appropriation of a policy on the use of genetically modified seeds, for example, and the network of actors and actants that might include groups of Kansas farmers and staff at the FAO, and most likely, representatives of agro-chemical corporations like Monsanto and activists with the Millions Against Monsanto movement. We assume that policy studies would benefit by tracing the processes by which actors and actants come into relationship with one another and form non-permanent assemblages aimed at producing, implementing, resisting, and appropriating policy to achieve particular aims.

- Comparison between countries often overemphasizes boundaries and treats nations as sovereign or as containers, when, in reality, international actors and institutions greatly influence national policy, especially in heavily-indebted countries. As in the example above, a country's agricultural policy may bear the seal of the national government but reflect the priorities of international organizations like the FAO, the World Trade Organization, and the World Bank, and of multinational corporations like Monsanto. We assume that national governments are receptive to global policy recommendations to varying degrees owing to the ways they are positioned within policy networks as a result of their differing degrees of economic and political power vis-à-vis international institutions.

With these assertions in mind, we now turn to consider two analytical strategies that promote the analysis of how actors and texts are connected vertically to the phenomenon of interest. These include actor network theory and critical discourse analysis.

Actor Network Theory

Actor network theory (ANT) seeks to explain the interactions of human and the non-human actors by tracing the non-permanent assemblages they form. In the case of policy studies, the people who develop and enact a policy, as well as the non-human policy itself and its attendant forms, tests, and documentation, are granted equal analytical significance, a process known as "generalized symmetry" aimed at the "levelling of *a priori* dualisms" in the study of any sociotechnical network (Brown, 2011, p. 25). True to the ethnomethodological tradition from which it emerged, ANT does not seek to provide a general theory of action, nor does it assume that actors are bound by particular categories before they enter established networks; rather, ANT is used to explain "the specific materializing processes through which policymaking actually works to animate educational knowledge, identities, and practices" (Fenwick & Edwards, 2011, p. 710).

As developed in the field of science and technology studies, most notably by Bruno Latour and his colleagues, ANT considers how, within networks, people and objects get invited, excluded, and enrolled; how linkages are established, shift, and dissolve; and how social acts curtail or facilitate future actions (Fenwick & Edwards, 2011). ANT has been taken up in a number of fields in recent decades, including education, geography, and organizational studies, as a way to guide the study of complex interactions among actors within a network rather than focusing on the pre-determined location (local, national, or global) they are assumed to inhabit within it. From this perspective, people, objects, and texts become vested and act, and in so doing produce networks—they become "enrolled" in them and are then "accountable" to the networks (Fenwick & Edwards, 2011, p. 8).

Actor network theory is ideally suited to the exploration of the vertical dimension of a comparative case study as it provides a rationale for and guidance on tracing spatially non-contiguous assemblages of human and non-human actors. If one follows actors as they interact horizontally across sites *and* as they move vertically across scales, as ANT demands, then the presumption of cultural or national boundedness that burdens much of the traditional case study research is mitigated. Similarly, we can combat the tendency in traditional case study research to treat the phenomenon of interest and the context in which it is situated as either the same thing or distinct; with ANT, one focuses on how phenomena and context come into being, and how they *are* interrelated (Sobe & Kowalczyk, 2014).

In this way, ANT can contribute to the production of network ethnography wherein the network is both a conceptual and a methodological tool that helps to develop historically-specific, spatially-aware analyses of social relations (Ball, 2016; Hogan, 2016). Network ethnography starts with the policy rather than a pre-determined context like a company or a rural community, and it follows the networks of actors and actants using methods commonly associated with ethnographic research, such as participant observation and interviewing. The aim, according to Ball (2016, p. 4) is to "map and build the network" by documenting the connections among actors. He put forward several questions that frame network ethnography, and these may be helpful for you to consider as well:

> What spaces do policies travel through on the way from one place to another? Who is it that is active in those spaces and who moves between them? How is space/are spaces reconfigured as policies move through it/them and how are policies changed as they move?
>
> (p. 4)

These are questions addressed in different ways in the two cases to follow.

Example 4.1: Establishing Vertical Linkages Using Actor Network Theory

Let us now return to the ethnography by Jill Koyama mentioned above, which (as is often the case) began as her dissertation. Koyama used ANT in a fruitful way to examine the No Child Left Behind policy and how it linked a wide range of national, state, and school-based actors in the process of "making failure pay" across the United States. Focusing on the production of *school failure*, she engaged in vertical comparison by showing how NCLB, a national policy, articulated with New York City policies and with school-specific programs aimed at improving student performance that were already in place when NCLB arrived. NCLB enlisted multiple actants through its nearly 600 regulations, and Koyama examined how they came together to form a policy network, rather than how the policy coerced or determined their actions. As she stated, "NCLB directs, but does not determine, the performance of activities enlisted across, and within, state and local levels to achieve certain goals, including leaving no child behind" (2010, p. 27).

One of the most insightful elements of Koyama's analysis concerns the connections among key actants at the federal, city, and school levels who were temporarily brought together in the formation of the NCLB policy network.[1] For example, she showed how NCLB, enacted in 2002, and Children First, a policy specific to New York City initiated in 2003, were both targeted at "failing schools" and both employed private services and market-based initiatives to change school governance structures by making principals more accountable for student improvement. Although federal and city leaders (especially multi-billionaire New York mayor Michael Bloomberg) at the time shared a similar view of the merits of the market to improve education, many school principals felt otherwise. Principals did not necessarily welcome the idea that they were being held even more accountable for students' progress each year and had to use private companies specified in these policies to make it happen (see also Koyama, 2014). The companies at the heart of NCLB provided supplemental educational services (SES), which were mandated by the policy as a way for students in Title 1 schools (schools with a high percentage of low-income students) to obtain additional academic assistance free of charge during times when school is not in session ("Description of supplemental education services," 2012). This move marks a significant change in the notion of public education, as Koyama pointed out: "By mandating failing schools to contract with private tutoring companies to provide afterschool tutoring, SES blurs the boundaries between government, schooling, and commerce and brings the associations between public and private entities to the fore" (2010, p. 6). Approximately 75 percent of the New York City principals interviewed expressed concerns that the cost of SES was negatively affecting the quality of services provided to students during the school day and after school. As one principal complained:

> Face it, schools don't want to give this money to multi-million dollar companies to do some elevated homework help. We know where we need the money and we aren't too happy that the feds [federal government] are telling us we need to give it to SES providers.
>
> (2010, p. 61)

Although principals across the U.S. may have faced similar dilemmas, the use of ANT as an element in Koyama's ethnographic analysis of the NCLB policy enabled her to create a detailed picture of how policy actors in New York City were acutely affected by the dual mandates of NCLB and Children First. These two policies, she contended, created a plethora of technologies like databases aimed at measuring and tracking student and school performance. These complex databases—non-human though they may be—designated certain schools and their principals as failures, with concomitant actions taken against them (see also Koyama, 2011). In explaining this process vis-à-vis ANT, Koyama put forth the following argument:

> Nonhuman objects, like NCLB, can be mobilized by human actors. Once linked to human actors, such nonhuman objects, which are often denied in cultural analysis, become an admittedly important part of culture. In fact, they join with human agents to create joint vectors of agency, and together, they do things. They mediate, they translate, and they get other entities to take action.
>
> (2010, p. 11)

This example is one of many in *Making Failure Pay* that shows how human and non-human actants *do* things, and compel others to do so as they become connected in the formation of a policy network. In this case, the policy mandate that schools provide supplemental educational services required principals to reallocate federal Title 1 monies to private, for-profit tutoring companies. It also meant that test scores and the databases in which they were recorded were actors in that they arbitrated between school principals anxious to show their schools were improving (and nervous about losing their own jobs), and city, state, and federal officials who needed to demonstrate to the public that they were not about to leave any child behind (see also Koyama, 2012). Tracing and interpreting such negotiations and interactions across different scales is essential to vertical comparison, and it is especially important for the analysis of policy.

Exercise 4.1 How Might You Design a Vertical Comparison Informed by Actor Network Theory?

Jill Koyama carried out an unconventional educational ethnography in that she did not focus on one site and the students and teachers in it. Instead, she focused on two related policies—No Child Left Behind and Children First—and the human and non-human actors working in schools, in private companies, and for the government who came together as a result of it. Thus, this work "expands the field of study to transactional spaces that transcend physical locations," and

(continued)

(continued)

it is to this end that she applied ANT as she engaged in her vertical comparison (2010, p. 7). This study illustrates what Ball refers to as network ethnography, a particularly productive way of thinking about the vertical axis in a comparative case study.

As you reflect on this vertical comparison and on ANT, the following questions may help you to apply this example to your own research project:

- What policies have shaped the phenomenon of interest to you? In Koyama's case, she was interested in school failure. Though produced at different scales, the influential and interrelated policies of NCLB and Children First illustrated a similar logic about accountability and markets to bolster student success. Are there similar policy pairings at different scales that might be relevant for you to examine?
- Whether your study does or does not have a strong policy component, how can vertical comparison that traces actors across scales and sites help you to understand the central phenomenon as processual, as something that is in the process of being made through the human and non-human actants that constitute it?
- Who or what are the primary actants that you imagine, at this point, you will want to understand more fully? In *Making Failure Pay*, the supplemental educational services companies, the NCLB policy, and school principals were some of the most important ones. Who or what might they be for your study?
    - If you do not agree with the basic tenet of ANT that non-human entities can have agency, can you still make use of this theory in your study? If so, how so?
    - What is your hunch—only an educated guess at this point—as to how these various actants at different scales may be coming together to form a network? Draw the emerging network of actants as you see it based on what you already know about the phenomenon of interest to you. Retain a copy of this diagram as part of your fieldnotes because you may find yourself returning to this initial diagram of your network and adding or pruning it as your research progresses. Remember, though, that the network is dynamic, and relationships you observe now may not endure; this process of mapping should be ongoing throughout the life of your research project.

Critical Discourse Analysis

Returning to our assumptions about vertical comparison, we find that case study research must be multi-scalar if it is to make claims about the phenomenon of interest that extend beyond a single, putatively-bounded site. Engaging in multi-scalar research means that one thinks there is something important happening that spans the local and the national, the national and the global, and that the researcher no longer sees these as binaries or as discrete levels.

Your goal, as a researcher, is to study interactions and trace connections. There are many ways that researchers analyze diverse texts to which actors in different social locations may be responding, and this section takes up one way that is particularly well-aligned with comparative case studies with a critical bent to them. This approach is called critical discourse analysis, or CDA, and it is ideally suited to the study of social practice, including the practice of policy as it is, by definition, a social text imbued with authority.

Critical discourse analysis invites us to consider how influential representations of certain groups of people, places, or issues come into being through language. It asserts that this is a form of power—the ability to exercise control over how something is represented—and that it is essential to understand in an era when direct coercion by dominant groups is increasingly risky to their interests (think here of how police violence can be captured on smart phones, circulated widely, and protested by organizations like Black Lives Matter). CDA assumes that there is a fundamental relationship between social structures in society and the discourse structures of influential texts, such as the speeches of political candidates, a national policy like NCLB, or even a widely circulated meme.

Policies are certainly not the only kinds of influential texts that can be analyzed using CDA. To return to the example in our introduction, corporate or university mission statements are also influential texts, as are media reports. However, policies are particularly ripe for such analysis because they do a great deal of representational work to establish problems— failing schools and inadequate annual assessment of students in the case of NCLB—and to categorize certain actors as part of these problems or as potential allies in solving them. Yet CDA does not assume that meaning is fixed or that representations do not change; rather, it submits that language and social practices "articulate" and "disarticulate" at different historical moments. In the process of being (re)articulated, discursive elements that have been brought together in a specific moment of practice are transformed, some achieving stabilization or permanence, others becoming disjunctive and ambiguous (Moretti & Pestre, 2015; Vavrus & Kwauk, 2013; Vavrus & Seghers, 2010).

Critical discourse analysis may sound a bit like actor network theory, and it should because they are ontologically similar. Both suggest there is no 'real' objective world out there for researchers to discover, as the ontology of objectivism would have it (Crotty, 1998). In ANT, for instance, networks are not assumed to exist prior to actors coming together to form them. As explained in *Making Failure Pay*:

> There is no stable presumption of the actor. The radical indeterminacy of the actor is a necessary element of the network. . . . What becomes significant is not dependent on actors as personalized positions, but as members of a network to which they are, even momentarily, accountable.
>
> (Koyama, 2010, p. 41)

Similarly, CDA starts with the constructionist (also called subjectivist or interpretivist) ontological position that social relations and social phenomena like written texts are always in the process of being reinscribed with meaning. As Christina Kwauk, whose dissertation we will explore below, and Frances Vavrus wrote in a policy analysis article, CDA

> assumes that the meaning of any signifying system, such as language, does not reside in objects or words themselves but rather that meanings are constructed by social actors in particular cultural and historical contexts . . . . This view does not deny the materiality of 'things' like school fees or conditions like poverty; rather, it presumes that objects and states are inscribed with meaning through socially produced signifying systems and practices that change over time.
>
> (Vavrus & Kwauk, 2013, pp. 352–353)

Thus, it makes sense to think about how you might use ANT and/or CDA in your comparative case study, but first let us look a bit more deeply at CDA.

As noted above, CDA is a way of examining how authoritative texts perform their ideological work. To do so, one needs to think simultaneously about the linguistic dimensions of texts and the representational dimensions that make certain kinds of texts authoritative in the first place during particular moments in time (Foucault, 2002). James Gee, a linguist who has helped to develop a certain strand of CDA, made a useful distinction between "discourse" ('little d') and "Discourse" ('big D') (2004). In this model, "discourse" is the rubric used to describe the linguistic features of oral and written texts, such as the lexicon, morphology, and syntax. "Discourse" with a capital D is used to connote broader socio-cultural and political contexts that shape the formation of texts and how to respond to them. Influenced by Foucault's discussion of power/knowledge, Ball asserted:

> Power and knowledge are two sides of a single process. Knowledge does not reflect power relations but is immanent in them. Discourses are, therefore, about what can be said, and thought, but also about who can speak, when, where and with what authority.
>
> (1990, p. 17)

The approach to CDA associated with Norman Fairclough, considered by many to be the founder of the field of critical linguistics, provides a complementary way of conceptualizing the discourse–Discourse relationship (1992, 2000, 2003). According to Fairclough, what Gee calls Discourse is discussed extensively in contemporary social theory—think about how often you have seen the phrases *educational discourse, policy discourse,* or *development discourse* in academic books and journal articles—but this theorizing does not adequately consider language in the 'little d' (discourse) sense. For Fairclough, a linguist by training, "there is a pervasive failure amongst social theorists to operationalize their theorisations of language in ways of showing specifically how language figures in social life within social research" (2000, p. 164). If one is to embrace CDA as Fairclough, Gee, and others have conceptualized it, then the study of discourse is essential to understanding Discourse (see also Van Leeuwen, 2007; Vavrus & Kwauk, 2013; Wodak, de Cillia, Reisigl, & Liebhart, 2000).

The most robust CDA projects examine three elements at once, namely, the lexical and syntactic structures (discourse) in a text, the processes of discourse production, and the dissemination and circulation of Discourse. Fairclough named each of these three dimensions of CDA: (1) *discourse-as-text*, the most 'micro' level of analysis of the linguistic building blocks of texts; (2) *discourse-as-discursive-practice*, the meso-level analysis of the production and distribution of texts; and (3) *discourse-as-social-practice*, the macro-level analysis of Discourse (2003). Thus, CDA attends simultaneously to linguistic elements in spoken or written texts, such as grammar, vocabulary, and cohesion, and to the broader socio-cultural and political context that shapes the formation of texts and how people think, feel, and act in response to them. In short, CDA engages researchers in a process of "revealing the relationship between linguistic means, forms and structures and concrete linguistic practice, and making transparent the reciprocal relationship between discursive action and political and institutional structures" (Wodak et al., 2000, p. 9). This is an especially useful approach for vertical comparison of policy because it links micro-level textual analysis with the macro-level exploration of how authoritative knowledge is generated and distributed by national and international policymaking institutions.

Example 4.2: Establishing Vertical Linkages
Using Critical Discourse Analysis

The compatibility of CDA and ethnography is not self-evident, but there have been a number of efforts in recent years to show how the two might be combined productively in a single study of policy (Johnson, 2011; Krzyzanowski, 2011). Christina Kwauk's dissertation (2014) offers an excellent example of how one might bring the two together in the study of policy networks. She went into greater detail in her use of CDA in an article using the same set of data (Kwauk, 2012), so we draw on both texts in this case study of the international sport for development movement and the policy networks that constitute it.

Kwauk spent a total of 12 months in Sāmoa studying the Discourse of Healthy Islands Through Sport, or HITS, as it has been constituted by actors across scales and sites, such as the Australian Sports Commission, the Sāmoan Ministry of Health, and in Sāmoan secondary schools. She considered how global policies regarding sport, development, and health have been formulated and disseminated across the Pacific by multiple actors and institutions, and have been appropriated by a range of actors on the islands that compose this archipelago. Her vertical comparison of policy and practice was informed by many of the CDA scholars mentioned above, most notably Gee (2005) and his Discourse/discourse pairing. For instance, she began her dissertation with a vignette describing the international Beyond Sport Summit she attended in Chicago, at which speakers insisted on the potential of sport to help countries in the global South meet the United Nations Millennium Development Goals, a set of eight goals for improving education, health, and especially economic development by 2015. Critical of such grand claims, Kwauk then laid out her central argument:

> Yet as this global big "D" discourse of sport for development is increasingly inscribed upon and re-produced by the local, it simultaneously threatens to crowd out alternative little "d" discourses of sport for development (cf. Gee, 2005). These little "d" discourses have emerged from local experiences of sport, conceptualizations of health, and visions of development that complicate international commonsense assumptions about the role that sport plays in improving people's lives.
>
> (2014, p. 4)

How did Kwauk support this claim that there is a disjuncture between global Discourse and local experience regarding sport and development? To represent this conceptually, she opted not to use the terms macro, meso, and micro and, instead, posits a framework that highlights the points of articulation between them by using *micro:meso* and *meso:macro* throughout her dissertation. Viewing sport for development as a policyscape as discussed in Chapter 1 (Carney, 2009), Kwauk provided her rationale for this conjoining of terms:

> Specifically, I 'followed' the concept of sport for development to compare the meanings of healthy living and development as they were (inter) discursively formulated and constructed by actors at the translocal (micro:meso) and inter/national (meso:macro) rungs of a sport for development policyscape. Each of these levels and the actors within them, while geographically spread, are in an ongoing relation with each other, creating fluid, hybrid, and evolving chains of ideas, terms, and images of sport and development.
>
> (2014, p. 36)

These relationships are captured in Figure 4.1, which serves as a visual depiction of these pivotal points in the development and appropriation of sport for development policy. The micro:meso analysis centered on the discourses and practices of people who participated in village-level sports groups, such as Village Sport Councils and youth groups, and those involved in setting

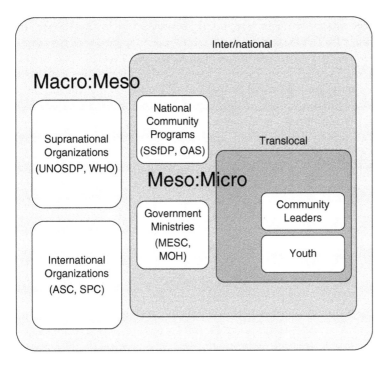

Figure 4.1 Christina Kwauk's Depiction of the Policy Actors in Her Study of Sport for Development.

and monitoring policy at the national level through the Sāmoan Ministry of Education, Sports and Culture (MESC) and its various efforts, including the Sāmoa Sports for Development Program (SSfDP). The meso:macro linkages were examined as Kwauk compared and contrasted national policies and programs and views of Sāmoan policy actors at the national level with those of international bodies like the Secretariat of the Pacific Community (SPC) and the World Health Organization (WHO). Kwauk summed up her framework as follows:

> This ... vertical and relational reconceptualization of the field provided me with a conceptual framework for seeing how 'local' artic-ulations of sport, health, and development in Sāmoa were situated within broader inter/national and translocal flows of material, money, and bodies.
>
> (2014, p. 39)

Kwauk used CDA in various ways in her research, but it was particularly useful in her analysis of policy discourse at the meso:macro juncture. She showed how this coming together of policy actors produces the HITS

Discourse that links high rates of non-communicable diseases related to obesity to economic collapse and moral disintegration in the Pacific. In the tradition of CDA, Kwauk did not ignore the materiality of the problem at hand, such as the prevalence of diabetes and heart disease in the region, but she noted that the focus on biomedical and individual aspects of these issues masks their political dimensions: "Technical language not only conceals the political nature of development project ideas, choices, and goals, but it also functions to de-author those who claim the inevitability of these threatening changes and to elide tougher debates that need further negotiation" (2014, p. 98). In this case, some of these "tougher debates" included where Sāmoa is located in global food chains that supply canned meat and other foods high in fat and sugar to the islands, and how global media promote narrow notions about beauty and body size that conflict with cultural views about *puta* (to be fat) and *pa'e'e* (to be skinny/scrawny) (2014, p. 393).

In Kwauk's research, she looked closely at international policies and frameworks that have shaped national sport and physical education policies in the Pacific and have helped to produce a central 'truth' in the Discourse of HITS: Sport as the main solution to the health crisis in Sāmoa. Even though national health policy also encouraged people to reduce alcohol consumption and cease smoking, sport was given particular prominence as a way to improve not only the physical body but also the collective national body that is languishing economically. In her dissertation, Kwauk honed in on texts produced by the Australian Sports Commission (ASC), which played an outsized role in sport policy and programming in Sāmoa, and she examined how the organization shifts the focus on sport for health to sport to address a broader array of social ills that the ASC identifies among its island neighbors. For example, ASC reports repeatedly used phrases describing sport as "socially engaging," "a convenor of people," an "effective tool for empowering youth and older women in developing countries," and as "easy, exciting, enjoyable, and everywhere" (cited in Kwauk, 2014, p. 102). These reports, according to Kwauk, also rely on what on CDA scholar Van Leeuwen (2007) calls the "language of legitimation" in policy, in which a set of particular policy interventions are legitimated due to the intensity of a crisis. The ASC texts represent, in various ways, the bodies of Pacific Islanders as abnormal and legitimate targets for intervention so as to produce physically and psychologically stronger persons:

> In contrast to the image of the sickly, immobile, and disempowered Pacific Islander, the HITS governing apparatus simultaneously attempts to inscribe a new (healthy) persona onto the bodies of Islanders: one that is productive, disciplined, and responsible. Strategically converging with its discourse on the power and goodness of sport, HITS discourse constructs an image of what Pacific Islanders could be like if

they participated in more sport and physical activity: they will "increase their ability to organise, lead, network, communicate, cooperate, self-determine, become more active and develop a sense of responsibility and fair play."

(ASC, 2011, p. 1, cited in Kwauk, 2014, p. 115)

By employing both biomedical discourse and a neoliberal discourse that 'individualizes' economic and social development, a broader sport for development Discourse is produced that has a global reach but seizes onto specific national and local 'crises' to help legitimize and mobilize it.

In her article, Kwauk used an even more refined set of CDA tools to examine three additional international policies and declarations on sport, health, and development that have affected policymaking in the Pacific. She developed a three-prong approach for her analysis, drawing on Fairclough (2001) and Greene (1999), and the following extended quote describes her primary strategies:

> I scanned the documents … looking specifically for collocated (or co-occurring) concepts, overwording, and the use of metaphors. Next, I used Fairclough's (2001) tools for interpretation and explanation of the texts to understand how the documents reflect an interaction between text (vocabulary) and ideology (of its producers), and between ideology and social orders. I re-read the documents for presuppositions and commonsense assumptions, paying specific attention to moments of disjuncture and ambiguity. Finally, I used Greene's (1999) invention, circulation, and regulation schemata to help guide my interpretation of the findings derived from the initial and second readings of the documents.… I continually referred back to the texts to locate any disconfirming discursive occurrences, as well as to delve deeper into a self-reflexive analysis of my own interpretive procedures and commonsense assumptions used to understand those of the authors of the documents I was analyzing.
>
> (2012, p. 43)

Although we cannot illustrate all of these strategies, several stand out for their relevance to the analysis of authoritative texts like policy. First, Kwauk showed how overwording, which indicates the intensity of an ideological struggle playing out in a text, was evident in the 2004 World Health Organization (WHO) policy on physical activity and health she included in her corpus. She found that, in the first three pages alone, the policy repeatedly uses words like "diet", "risk factors," and "burden"—up to 14 times in the case of "burden," for example.

Second, Kwauk looked at the use of metaphor, a particularly powerful discursive strategy in that it profoundly shapes our view of social reality owing to its cognitive and affective dimensions (Guo, 2013). In the case of the WHO policy, Kwauk showed how it relies on the "value-heavy metaphor of the 'burden of disease,'" which she argued helped to link the domains of health and economics:

> 'burden' (burden of disease, disease burden) is both an economic and social burden for governments and families who must pay a price (figuratively and literally) to care for those who are not healthy. The use of the term 'disease' works then to medicalize fatness and to transform obese bodies into diseased bodies ....
>
> (2012, p. 45)

Third, Kwauk discussed the process of regulation, which in this case has to do with maintenance of obesity as a "rhetorical controversy" (p. 48). She explored the way that the collocation of three key term—diet, physical activity, and health—worked to naturalize them as biomedical solutions to the 'crisis' of obesity in the Pacific and positions them as "politically neutral, socially (and biologically) natural, and outside the realm of ideology" (2012, p. 49). Regulation, one of several important processes by which ideology is maintained, can be studied systematically through the analysis of influential international texts as well as authoritative documents produced domestically and at much smaller scales such as schools in Sāmoa. Through the use of multiple analytical strategies, including but not limited to these three, Kwauk built an effective argument about the co-production of the Discourse of HITS and the discourses by which it is constituted.

Exercise 4.2 How Might You Use CDA in Your Vertical Comparison?

Christina Kwauk's ethnography of the Healthy Island Through Sport Discourse focused specifically on Sāmoa but included research in other countries— including the U.S.—because she wanted to understand how particular 'truths' about health and sport have been conveyed through global Discourse. Like Jill Koyama, Kwauk's study spanned locations and used a variety of research methods, including CDA.

Think about the following questions in relations to Kwauk's study and your own as you consider how CDA may be used to enhance your analysis of texts produced at macro, meso, and macro levels (or macro:meso and meso:micro junctures as Kwauk suggested).

- Taking each of the terms in CDA in turn—*discourse-as-text, discourse-as-discursive-practice*, and *discourse-as-social-practice*—what makes this approach to discourse analysis *critical* in the sense of critical theory discussed in Chapter 2?

  o If you do not see yourself as a critical scholar or do not view your research as making an intervention to interrupt oppressive social relations, do the techniques of CDA still make sense? Why or why not?

Make a list of the texts (e.g., policies, mission statements, media) produced by others that you have gathered or will gather that are relevant to your study.

- What approach might be best to analyze these, and why? For example, might CDA, discourse analysis, conversation analysis, or content analysis be best, and why?
  - How might you analyze them in terms of 'little d' discourse?
  - How might you compare these texts vertically to make an argument that a particular Discourse is relevant to the phenomenon of central interest to you?
- What are the different types of texts that your study is likely to generate (interview transcripts, fieldnotes, etc.)? Will you analyze those documents linguistically? If so, how?

Conclusion

In this chapter, we presented the vertical axis of the comparative case study. We showed how tracing associations, networks, and phenomena across scales can interrupt traditional notions of context and culture, frame the broader sociopolitical and economic contexts of relevance, and follow the inquiry. We explained how actor network theory informs vertical comparison and then examined Jill Koyama's exemplary book, *Making Failure Pay*, as an example of a vertical comparison of educational policies. We then reviewed the method of critical discourse analysis and considered how Christina Kwauk skillfully used it to explore the global sport for development movement and how it is manifested through policies affecting everyday lives in Sāmoa. In both cases, we hinted at how Koyama and Kwauk masterfully integrated both vertical and horizontal comparisons to the benefit of their studies.

In the next chapter, we turn to the final axis—the transversal—to demonstrate how a historical perspective on comparison can further enhance social research.

Note

1 NCLB was replaced in 2015 with a new national policy, the Every Student Succeeds Act.

References

Ball, S. J. (1990). *Politics and policy making in education: Explorations in sociology.* New York: Routledge.
Ball, S. J. (2016). Following policy: Networks, network ethnography and education policy mobilities. *Journal of Education Policy.* DOI: 10.1080/02680939.2015.1122232.

Brown, S. D. (2011). Actor-network theory. In M. Tadajewski, P. Maclaran, E. Parsons, & M. Parker (Eds.), *Key concepts in critical management studies* (pp. 24–28). London & Thousand Oaks, CA: Sage.

Carney, S. (2009). Negotiating policy in an age of globalization: Exploring educational "policyscapes" in Denmark, Nepal, and China. *Comparative Education Review* 53(1), 63–88.

Crotty, M. (1998). *The foundations of social research*. Thousand Oaks, CA: Sage.

Description of supplemental educational services. (2012). Available at http://www2.ed.gov/nclb/choice/help/ses/description.html.

Fairclough, N. (1992). *Discourse and social change*. Cambridge: Polity Press.

Fairclough, N. (2000). Discourse, social theory, and social research: The discourse of welfare reform. *Journal of Sociolinguistics* 4(2), 163–195.

Fairclough, N. (2001). *Language and power* (2nd ed.). Harlow, UK: Longman.

Fairclough, N. (2003). "Political correctness": The politics of culture and language. *Discourse and Society* 14(1), 17–28.

Fenwick, T., & Edwards, R. (2011) *Actor-network theory in education*. New York: Routledge.

Foucault, M. (2002). *The order of things: An archaeology of the human sciences*. London: Routledge. (Original work published in 1966.)

Gardinier, M. (2012). Agents of change and continuity: The pivotal role of teachers in Albanian educational reform and democratization. *Comparative Education Review* 56(4), 659–683.

Gardinier, M. (2014). Middlemen and midwives of reform: The in-between worlds of Albanian educational policy-makers and professionals. *Comparative Education* 51(2), 276–292.

Gee, J. P. (2004). Discourse analysis: What makes it critical? In R. Rogers (Ed.), *An introduction to critical discourse analysis in education* (pp. 19–50). Mahwah, NJ: Lawrence Erlbaum Associates.

Gee, J. P. (2005). *An introduction to discourse analysis: Theory and method* (2nd ed.). New York and London: Routledge.

Greene, R. W. (1999). *Malthusian worlds: U.S. leadership and the governing of the population crisis*. Boulder, CO: Westview Press.

Guo, S. (2013). Metaphor studies from the perspective of critical discourse analysis: A case study of business acquisition. *Theory and Practice in Language Studies* 3(3), 475–481.

Hogan, A. (2016). Network ethnography and the cyberflâneur: Evolving policy sociology in education. *International Journal of Qualitative Studies in Education* 29(3), 381–398.

Johnson, D. C. (2011). Critical discourse analysis and the ethnography of language policy. *Critical Discourse Studies* 8(4), 267–279.

Koyama, J. (2010). *Making failure pay: For-profit tutoring, high stakes testing, and public schools*. Chicago: University of Chicago Press.

Koyama, J. (2011). Generating, comparing, manipulating, categorizing, reporting, and sometimes fabricating data to comply with No Child Left Behind mandates. *Journal of Education Policy* 26(5), 701–720.

Koyama, J. (2012). Making failure matter: Enacting No Child Left Behind's standards, accountabilities, and classifications. *Educational Policy* 26(6), 870–891.

Koyama, J. (2014). Principals as bricoleurs: Making sense of data and making do in an era of accountability. *Educational Administration Quarterly* 50(2), 279–304.

Krzyzanowski, M. (2011). Ethnography and critical discourse analysis: Towards a problem-oriented research dialogue. *Critical Discourse Studies 8*(4), 231–238.

Kwauk, C. (2012). Obesity and the healthy living apparatus: Discursive strategies and the struggle for power. *Critical Discourse Studies 9*(1), 39–57.

Kwauk, C. (2014). Playing for the future: Sport and the production of healthy bodies in policy and practice (unpublished dissertation). University of Minnesota, Twin Cities.

Leander, K., & Sheehy, M. (Eds.). (2004). *Spatializing literacy research and practice*. New York: Peter Lang.

Moretti, F., & Pestre, D. (2015). Bankspeak: The language of World Bank reports. *New Left Review 92*, 75–99.

Sobe, N. W., & Kowalczyk, J. A. (2014). Exploding the cube: Revisioning "context" in the field of comparative education. *Current Issues in Comparative Education 16*(1), 6–12.

Van Leeuwen, T. (2007). Legitimation in discourse and communication. *Discourse & Communication 1*(1), 91–112.

Vavrus, F., & Kwauk, C. (2013). The new abolitionists? The World Bank and the "boldness" of global school fee elimination reforms. *Discourse: Studies in the Cultural Politics of Education 34*(3), 351–365.

Vavrus, F., & Seghers, M. (2010). Critical discourse analysis in comparative education: A discursive study of "partnership" in Tanzania's poverty reduction policies. *Comparative Education Review 54*(1), 77–103.

Wodak, R., de Cillia, R., Reisigl, M., & Liebhart, K. (2000). *The discursive construction of national identity*. Edinburgh: Edinburgh University Press.

5   Tracing the Transversal

We come at last to the transversal. As we have already noted, the transversal axis connects the horizontal elements to one another *and* to the vertical scales to study across and through a phenomenon as a way of exploring how it has changed over time. We have argued throughout this book that we need new ways of studying interconnections across dispersed locations that include examining multiple sites at the same scale—such as three schools or NGOs in the same city—and across scales to understand how School A may be configured differently from Schools B and C. There are many reasons why this might be the case, but one may be historical differences in linkages to state officials or in the ways that national policy has been appropriated by those in School A compared to its neighboring schools.

We have also maintained that traditional case study research has not adequately attended to historical work. Yin (2014), we believe, drew too stark a distinction between present and past in suggesting that the phenomenon of central concern be "contemporary" because he contended that "events extending back to the 'dead' past" cannot be studied through interviews and observations (p. 24). Other advocates of case study methods have also largely ignored historical elements. Although observation and interviewing are often very useful research methods, we aver that sense-making by researchers studying contemporary phenomena should include comparisons across contemporary sites and scales, *and* over time. We have seen repeatedly in the cases explored in this volume that actants who appear similar in some ways are enlisted in social networks, especially policy networks, to different degrees and move into and out of them at different historical moments; it is the temporal study of these changing assemblages across sites and scales that we mean by tracing the transversal.

In this chapter, we discuss an array of methods that can be used for transversal analysis and several extended examples, including our own longitudinal research, to illustrate the importance of temporal study.[1] These include life histories, oral histories, archival research, and surveying because these are the methods we have found most beneficial in our research and in the work of others using a CCS approach. We first provide an overview of these methods and identify sources that provide much greater detail on them. We then discuss studies that draw upon different combinations of these methods as part of qualitative or mixed methods longitudinal projects. Throughout, we pose questions to help you think about the transversal dimension of the phenomenon that interests you. First, however, we outline central assumptions that inform a transversal comparison, followed by the examination of several illustrative cases.

Transversal Comparison: Central Assumptions

The previous chapters focused on horizontal and vertical comparisons. In each case, we mentioned examples of studies that also incorporated historical analysis by way of previewing how to integrate transversal perspectives. Here, we briefly review key premises that inform the transversal axis: [2]

- Social phenomena of concern to us today have historical roots. For example, racial disparities in education in the U.S. reflect centuries of systematic underfunding of schools for people of color and the political machinations that have allowed for the perpetuation of separate districts and schools and of performance-based tracking. Similarly, colonialism as practiced by the U.S. and European powers continues to reverberate into the present, affecting economic relations and social issues such as migration and educational opportunities. We believe that the study of any contemporary issue needs to go back in time to understand how it came to be in the first place.
- History offers an extensive fount of evidence regarding how social institutions function and how social relations are similar and different around the world. Historical analysis provides an essential opportunity to contrast how things have changed over time and to consider what has remained the same in one locale or across much broader scales. Such historical comparison reveals important insights about the flexible cultural, social, political, and economic systems humans have developed and sustained over time.
- Time and space are closely connected. Returning to the example of racial disparities in U.S. education, we can consider how, over the course of many years, wealth gaps have grown between black and white communities owing to a range of factors, including disparities in home ownership, federal policies that redlined people in predominantly black neighborhoods, and discriminatory lending; unequal schooling; and inequalities in the labor market, including employment discrimination. When funding for schooling is tied to local property taxes, schools in wealthier—and typically whiter—districts have more resources. Thus, spatial disparities in housing are linked to geographically disparate access to well-funded schools, and these differences have accumulated over time.

- The study of history allows us to assess evidence and conflicting interpretations of a phenomenon, heightening our ability to question assumptions about the shape and form it has taken in the contemporary era. Too often, researchers take for granted the ways institutions operate today rather than looking at them analytically through a historical lens. For instance, classrooms segregated by age may seem 'natural' in the U.S. today, but the history of U.S. education shows that this organizational system was not inevitable and that schools could have been organized—and are organized around the world—in other ways. Thus, the study of change and constancy over time opens up alternative explanations for phenomena that may seem self-evident if examined only from a contemporary perspective.

Methods for Developing the Transversal Axis: Longitudinal Research

As we have seen in previous chapters, there are many ways of looking at change over time in a comparative case study. This might involve focus group discussions and actor network analysis, and so, too, the four methods we focus on in this section: life histories, oral histories, archival research, and surveying. Although some of the scholars discussed in the previous chapters used these methods, we have not discussed them extensively or shown how they can be used alone or in combination with other methods to analyze the temporal dimension of a CCS.

Life Histories and Oral Histories

Life histories and oral histories are, in many respects, quite similar. Here we include both, though specialists might wish to distinguish them. Life history interviews have been an important tool for anthropologists since the foundation of the field. Some of the earliest, and most famous, life histories were conducted with Native Americans.[3] Life history methods grew to fame for their use by Chicago School sociologists in the 1920s and 1930s to document life in urban environments. The resulting studies gave insights into the lives of particular people and how larger social structures influenced their life stories (e.g., Anderson, 1923; Shaw, 1930; Cornwell & Sutherland, 1937). Though life history methods were marginalized by the rise of quantitative methods in sociology, and to a lesser degree by the emphasis on observation demonstrated by those invested in social interactionism and ethnomethodology, they continued to be used by some social scientists throughout the twentieth century. Life histories featured centrally in influential anthropological studies of the 1960s, such as Marjorie Shostak's *Nisa* (1961) and Oscar Lewis's *The Children of Sanchez* (1961). Feminist researchers, in particular, value life history methods for their ability to give participants more control over interactions and to make the experiences of ordinary people more central to research (Goodson, 2001; see also Maynes, Pierce, & Laslet, 2012). These methods of interviewing also appeal to those who distrust cultural analyses that have oversimplified groups and presented coherent, static cultures, because they highlight the different ways that lives among a putatively similar group of people are lived. In addition, life histories raise fascinating questions about the phenomenological process of comparing oneself to others and of blending the perceptions of investigator and subject/participant (Frank, 1979). Life history methods are also attractive to scholars influenced by post-structuralism whose emphasis on subjectivities moves them away from modernist master narratives, even as some have questioned the tendency of life histories to suggest a linearity, teleology, and coherence that would make post-structuralist scholars skeptical (Munro, 1998).

The 1990s witnessed an efflorescence of life history research, particularly by feminist scholars whose interests lay in the ways that individuals use narrative to make sense of their lives. By focusing on "cultural scripts and narrative devices," research using life history "emphasizes the *truth of the telling versus telling the truth*" (Frank, 1995, p. 145, emphasis ours; see also Linde, 1993 and Rosenwald & Ochberg, 1992).

Ruth Behar's *Translated Woman: Crossing the Border with Esperanza's Story* (2003) provides an eloquent example of the power of life history methods. Using narrative techniques more characteristic of novels than life histories, *Translated Woman* tells the story of Esperanza Hernandez, an iconoclastic woman from Mexquitic, 500 miles south of the U.S. border. Esperanza experienced significant abuse as a child and later as a wife, as well as extreme deprivation and the loss of many children. She vividly describes the *coraje* that propelled her to leave her husband and become a street peddlar to support herself and her children. Refusing to assume traditional gender roles, Esperanza confronted her husband's lover, harshly judged her own children, and ended up socially outcast, considered by many to be a 'witch.' Esperanza found redemption in a spiritist cult directed by an androgynous leader and built around Pancho Villa, the Mexican Revolutionary hero. In the controversial final chapter to the book, the anthropologist Behar drew parallels to her own life as a Jewish Cuban immigrant to the U.S. She described the pain of being mistreated and underestimated by her own father, as well as by her teachers. The resulting book caused quite a stir in anthropology when it was first published because of the questions it raised about voice, anthropological representations, privilege, the possibilities and limits of relationships forged during fieldwork, and the ability to know others who are fundamentally different from ourselves.

Oral history represents an effort to broaden individual life histories because it uses interviews with various individuals and families, not one person's story alone, to document memories of important events or processes. For example, in his poignant oral history of a 1944 Nazi massacre of 335 unarmed civilians in Rome, Portelli (2003) draws on oral histories with relatives of the victims, survivors, and partisans who fought the Nazis to consider the struggle for freedom under fascism. Oral historians generally endeavor to obtain information from different perspectives, and they often complement these sources with archival materials. For example, Kathy Davis's (2007) book, *The Making of Our Bodies, Ourselves: How Feminism Travels across Borders*, used the Boston Women's Health Book Collective's records at the Schlesinger Library, as well as interviews and focus groups with collective members and staff, to document the evolution of the landmark volume on women's bodies and sexuality. It then relied on interviews with translators, focused on the Latin American and Bulgarian versions, to look at how the volume was not only translated but transformed as it was internationalized. Davis emphasized the book's epistemology, which encouraged women to use their own experiences as knowledge resources, as the basis for its broad and revolutionary appeal and its success in avoiding the imposition of U.S. feminist ideologies.

Oral history, of course, involves a complex set of analytical and ethical issues. There are lively debates over processes of interpretation; whether the approach should more closely resemble art or social science; how theory influences method; the politics of representation; reporting and interpreting memories; transcription; the role of audio- and video-recording; legal ramifications; and ethical considerations, among many others (see Ritchie, 2011; Perks & Thomson, 1998; Sheftel & Zembrzycki, 2013; Cave & Sloan, 2014). Nonetheless, life history and oral history offer fruitful approaches to including a transversal element in a research project.[4]

Archival Research

Archival research is a way of helping to identify the historical forces that have shaped the phenomenon of interest in a study. We can think of an archive as a collection of primary sources, such as personal letters, photographs, films, minutes of meetings, official correspondence, and reports, with some archives being freestanding institutions and others located in the special collections section of a library. In working with archived materials, there are both political and practical considerations that affect how one conducts historical research and writes about the available sources.

Regarding the politics of the archive, it is important to keep in mind that what is catalogued and kept in an archive is never neutral and can, in fact, be highly contentious (Derrida & Prenowitz, 1995; Gandhi, 1998; Manoff, 2004). This is because the materials in an archive had to have been deemed important to save, and it is generally the papers of more powerful individuals that are collected and catalogued. Moreover, people who cannot write for whatever reason tend not to have such records, so there is not equal documentation of the lives of people regardless of class, gender, and race. In earlier eras, there was a sense that the archivist served as the neutral conduit through which unfiltered historical facts flowed from the materials s/he collected to the historian who read, recorded, and wrote about them. Today, historians' general rejection of positivism's certainty about the truth being 'out there' to be discovered has generated great interest in studying archivists and the archive. As Dodge explained:

> We cannot ever know 'what really happened' in spite of the obdurate belief of some who cling to the positivist view that we could know, if we just spent enough time sitting in that reading room wrenching the truth out of hapless documents by applying an objective, rational eye to them; who cling to the view that the documents and records chosen by, and in the custody of, the archivist, are objective, immutable relics which have a direct, unmediated correlation to the past, and, which once discovered by the historian and fully contextualized, can be arranged as an accurate reconstruction of the past.
>
> (2006, p. 346)

In addition to the politics of the archive, there are also practical considerations to using them. One of the frustrating—or liberating—aspects of archival research is that there is no agreed upon method for doing it. In fact, some historians do not believe that we can teach others how to 'do history' at all; rather, students should be given examples of well-written historical studies and carefully examine these exemplars in the field (Domanska, 2008). There are, though, a number of useful textbooks that include sections on, or are devoted to, archival research (Claus & Marriott, 2012; Ramsey, Sharer, L'Eplattenier, & Mastrangelo, 2010), but they are not 'how to' books as one finds in the case of survey research (see below). We offer a few recommendations for those who believe archival research might enhance the development of the transversal axis in their comparative case study while acknowledging that this is not an exhaustive list of suggestions.

Beginning with a rather obvious point, it is essential to create a system of cataloguing the materials you find because you will need to cite them so that you and others may locate them again in the archive. Unlike more familiar citation systems in the social sciences like the American Psychological Association (APA) format, archived materials often need to have more details recorded, such as a file number or a box number, or the author *and* the recipient of a letter to distinguish it from another letter written by the same person on the same date. Cataloguing can be done in a variety of ways, with the old index card system having given way in most cases to reference management software programs like Endnote or Zotero. The important point from our experience is not so much the technology one uses as it is the careful recording of details about each documents and even the sections within them to facilitate easy review and retrieval.

In addition, we recommend that you consider how you might preserve the materials you find, because many archives around the world do not receive adequate funding to maintain documents properly. Thus, paper starts to disintegrate, and files may be misplaced or lost altogether between one visit to an archive and the next, which, for a longitudinal project, may be many years apart. The photocopies or digital images that you make may become one of the only sources of these materials in the future, making the preservation of documents an important act of academic stewardship.

Finally, we recommend that you do a great deal of memoing—writing of notes to yourself—to help you think about the ways that the archival material you find might help you develop a temporal understanding of the phenomenon of interest to you. For example, you may be able to find a great deal of information online or in your university's library about contemporary educational policies to promote literacy in Tanzania, but how might your understanding of these policies change if you were to find in the Tanzania National Archives letters and reports by departing British colonial officials documenting previous efforts to bolster literacy or previous literacy policies by the government of independent Tanzania? It may not be immediately apparent to you as you read through the first few files on the topic, but you may, over time, develop a theory of how present and past literacy efforts resemble each other, leading to questions about how new or novel current approaches to bolstering literacy may be.

Surveying

In contrast to archival research, surveying requires that one's informants still be living, and research methods tend to be quite precise. There are many useful guides to survey design and analysis (Fowler, 2013; Groves et al., 2009), with most of them focusing on how to gather quantitative information about a group of people thought to share key attributes with a larger population of interest. For this reason, survey research is usually variable-oriented rather than process-oriented (see Chapter 2) as it is well designed to help us understand how variation in variable A co-occurs with variation in variable B. For example, a researcher might want to know how income level and philanthropy are related, and so s/he might administer a survey to a stratified random sample of residents in a city who are stratified by their monthly earnings but sampled randomly within each strata.

In the case of the CCS approach, surveying might be useful in comparing horizontally, vertically, or transversally. We could consider using a survey to study employees in four different technology start-up companies in Silicon Valley, for instance, whose parental leave policies vary widely. We could also administer a survey to a randomly selected group of high-school students in San Francisco who are enrolled in technology courses and to managers in technology companies across northern California to compare how different demographic and educational attributes correlate with perceptions of 'workplace readiness.' We include surveying in this chapter on the transversal axis because we believe surveys are an under-utilized method in comparing a phenomenon over time, as seen in Example 5.2 below. If a researcher wants to understand whether adherence to a national policy or access to a key social institution is increasing or decreasing, then it is possible to design survey questions that help to establish this temporal dimension of a study.

In addition to quantitative surveys, there are also qualitative surveys that enable researchers to study a process or policy but across a larger population than interviewing or observing would typically allow. Hansen (2010) argued that qualitative surveying has been largely ignored in the social sciences: "Surprisingly, the term *qualitative survey* (and/or the alternative diversity survey) is almost non-existent both in textbooks on general social research methodology … and in textbooks on qualitative research methods" (para. 7). She contrasted quantitative and qualitative surveys based primarily on the difference between seeking to know how something is *distributed* across a population, such as years of schooling or access to health care (quantitative survey) compared to finding out how much *diversity* there is in the population, e.g. in relation to their perspectives on or experience with schooling, health care, and the like (qualitative survey). Hansen noted that a qualitative survey might include some forced-choice items as one typically finds in a quantitative survey but would also have open-ended questions where participants can elaborate on their views. Moreover, these surveys typically differ from quantitative surveys in that the questions often emerge after an initial phase of qualitative research, such as six months into an ethnographic study, when the researcher has developed some initial categories and explanations that s/he wants to explore among a larger population.

In an exemplary longitudinal study that employed both ethnography and survey research, Peter Demerath and his colleagues studied the myriad ways that the phenomenon of *academic success* is produced in U.S. high schools (Demerath, 2009; Demerath, Lynch, Milner, Peters, & Davidson, 2010). During their four-year ethnographic study, they developed a "grounded survey," which emerged from their intensive study of one middle-class high school in a suburban community in the Midwest. They developed closed items on the survey that allowed them to examine correlations between variables they thought might be significant for their analysis, such as students' socioeconomic status and their grade point average. They also created open-ended questions that enabled them to get input from more students than they could have by conducting interviews alone ($N = 605$). The questions included items like the following: "How are you preparing to gain admission to the college of your choice?" (2010, pp. 2962–2963), and "Do you think you know better than your teachers how you ought to learn?" (p. 2966). By grounding the survey in their ongoing ethnographic fieldwork and using both quantitative and qualitative analysis in it, Demerath and his fellow researchers created a contextually meaningful research instrument that allowed them to gauge the circumstances and perspectives of a significant student population without losing any of the richness of the larger ethnography.

Exercise 5.1 How Might You Engage Methods to Focus on Change Over Time?

The methods outlined above give you a sense of the different ways you might examine how the phenomenon of interest to you has changed over time. This might be by conducting life history and/or oral history interviews; analyzing letters, reports, and policies in archives; or carrying out surveys of a cohort of people whom you may be able to follow over time as they move along a critical stage (or stages) in the life course. We encourage you to consider the antecedents of contemporary phenomena and the processes through which social problems have developed.

- What are the main historical forces that you suspect most influence the phenomenon at the center of your study? These might include things such as patterns of migration, social policy, employment opportunities, and the like.
- What research methods might you use to study those forces, including but not limited to the ones discussed above?
- What is a research question relevant to your project that could be answered using the historical method you listed above?
- How would an historical analysis of the central phenomenon in your study fit with the other components of your study? What new knowledge or additional comparative perspectives might you gain?

Integrating Methods in Qualitative Longitudinal Studies

Qualitative longitudinal studies engage core qualitative methodological techniques, such as interviews and observations, to understand how processes unfold over a long period of time. They also often use life history or oral history interviews and grounded surveys as Demerath and his colleagues employed (2010). These studies may be designed to follow a cohort during a milestone period in the life course, such as the high-school years, or they may be a *restudy* where the same or another researcher re-interviews some the same people many years after the initial study was completed (e.g., Burton, Purvin, & Garrett-Peters, 2009). There is little consensus in the field over what constitutes a sufficient period of time for a study to be considered 'longitudinal.' Saldaña (2003) joked that it requires simply a "lonnnnnnng time" (p. 1). How long is long, or long enough, depends on the research project, but the rationale for such a study is typically the same: longitudinal research is necessary when you want to understand how particular actions and interactions are situated temporally and remain constant or, more commonly, change over time.

Compton-Lilly (2015), a literacy scholar who has made excellent use of qualitative longitudinal methods, helpfully described four purposes of longitudinal research: (1) offering "contextual depth"; (2) examining "change over time"; (3) tracing "trajectories within institutional settings"; and (4) considering the "construction of ways of being over time" (pp. 223–227).

In her own work, Compton-Lilly (2003, 2007, 2012) followed a group of urban students from first grade through high school and examined the understandings about reading that these students brought to classrooms and how their attitudes changed over time as they progressed through school. Her ten-year longitudinal study included interviews with parents, students, and teachers, observations at school and (later) work, and the collection and analysis of school and art work by students, photos, and journals. This close examination of the same cohort of students over time enabled Compton-Lilly to describe quite specifically how educational institutional settings and socioeconomic factors shape students attitudes towards reading, their reading experiences, and their educational outcomes.[4]

Two excellent examples of restudying the same community or group come from Lois Weis (2004) and John Laub and Robert Sampson (2003). In the late 1980s, educational sociologist Weis (1990) conducted a rich ethnography of the students and teachers at Freeway High School, a predominantly white, working-class school in the northeastern Rust Belt. Specifically, she worked closely with 40 young white working-class men and women in their third year of high school, during a period of de-industrialization, the decline of the U.S. labor movement, and the emergence of the New Right. Fifteen years later, she returned to follow up with the participants, who were by then in their early thirties. Her comparison across time, developed in her monograph *Class Reunion* (2004), examined how neoliberal political and economic conditions in the U.S., the region, and (more specifically) the state and town have reshaped race, class, and gender identities, resulting in "a *distinct class* fraction, one distanced in key ways from other parts of what might be considered a broader working class" (p. 6). Weis asserted that, in 1985, white working-class identity derived from patriarchal expectations of home and family life and racist beliefs about African Americans and immigrant populations. Yet, she noted, the high-school girls "do not embrace the fantasies that they will be taken care of by the men in their lives" (p. 52), and, for this reason, these young women were adamant about getting jobs of their own. By 2000, Weis found, the majority of the women were married, and almost half had earned a university degree. In contrast, the story for the men was more mixed. Those chasing dwindling industrial employment were struggling. Those who had not only accepted service jobs (which they viewed as more 'feminine'), but also eschewed their idea of a wife at home and instead partnered with women who earned solid salaries, experienced greater stability and less hardship. Weis wrote, "It is those men who are willing and able to transgress the constructed working-class gender categories and valued masculinity of their high school youth for whom the new economy can produce 'settled lives'" (2004, p. 92). Thus, she demonstrated through this restudy how male members of the white working class sustained their economic standing by relying on women's demands for economic and educational opportunities. At the same time, Weis documented how racial positioning vis-à-vis African-Americans and immigrants remains central to the white working-class identities of her participants.

By conducting this restudy, Weis was able to trace how deindustrialization had, over time, influenced gender relations, economic opportunities, and racial identity formation. This beneficial approach illuminated the decidedly gendered paths that the young people had pursued. Weis was candid about the challenges of such work: she described the difficulties of tracking down the people from the original study and convincing skeptics to participate in the follow-up. Nonetheless, her results demonstrate the value of longitudinal methods in social research.

Laub and Sampson's *Shared Beginnings, Divergent Lives* (2003) is an extraordinary book which shows the deep insights gained by studying the whole life course, beginning in childhood and ending in later life. This restudy looked into the "the mechanisms underlying the processes of persistent offending and desistance from crime" (p. 38) by reinterviewing a group of men who had been part of a study conducted in the 1940s by Sheldon and Eleanor Glueck. They studied a sample of 500 Boston men (born 1925–1935) who were remanded to reform school. Between 1940 and 1965 the Gluecks collected a mass of data from these young men, who were interviewed at an average age of 14, again at 25, and finally at 32; they published the results in *Unravelling Juvenile Delinquency* (1950) and subsequent works. Many years later, sociologists Laub and Sampson conducted extensive state and national criminal history record searches and death records searches to find these same men. These data were complemented with life history interviews of the 52 men found, who by that time were in their sixties, using a stratified sampling technique. The resulting study vividly illuminates the sources of desistance from, and persistence in, crime over the men's lifetimes. Those interviewed identified four major turning points for desistance: marriage, military service, reform school, and neighborhood change. Laub and Sampson found that men who desisted from crime following their experience in reform school were rooted in structural routines and had strong social ties to family and community. The authors showed that, though the full life course matters immensely, it is rarely studied, and they make a make a clear case for the value of longitudinal studies.

This fascinating study by Laub and Sampson provides unique insights into the phenomenon of juvenile delinquency, and it also draws attention to the challenges of longitudinal research, particularly a restudy when many years have passed between research periods. It clearly requires patience and persistence, and this is becoming more difficult for researchers who are experiencing ever greater pressure to obtain fast results and publish them quickly. Further, when participants move, as they are likely to do over the course of decades, then a great deal of time is needed to locate them and travel costs mount to conduct follow-up interviews. There are also important methodological considerations as well, as documented in a range of methods texts (e.g., Neale & Flowerdew, 2003; Saldaña, 2003; Holland, 2007; Holland, Thomson, & Henderson, 2006). For example, careful planning is essential in order to build into your interview guide prospective questions, so you will not simply rely on retrospective comments. Thus, those who are intrigued by qualitative longitudinal work may wish to read the methods literature in this area as well as studies that engage the method. In what follows, we offer an extended example of a qualitative longitudinal study of our own to show how it addresses the transversal axis.

Example 5.1: Tracing the Transversal in a Qualitative Longitudinal Study at a Bilingual High School in New York City

In the monograph *Additive Schooling in Subtractive Times: Bilingual Education and Dominican Immigrant Youth in the Heights* (2011), Lesley Bartlett and Ofelia García worked with a team of researchers[5] to document the unusually successful efforts of one New York City high school to educate Dominican newcomer immigrant youth at a time when Latino immigrants constituted a growing and vulnerable population in the nation's secondary schools. We (Lesley and Ofelia) engaged in four and a half years of qualitative research at Gregorio Luperon High School in the neighborhood of Washington Heights in Manhattan to explore how the school staff and faculty supported students academically, socially, and linguistically. Drawing on classroom observations, interviews with administrators, faculty, students, parents, and founders, and focus groups with young people, we described how the school establishes and maintains strong relationships with students and their families, and how it utilizes a culturally-sustaining pedagogy to enact a dynamic bilingual approach that helps students develop academic Spanish and English.

The book traced the transversal axis of additive bilingual education in two ways. First, it attended to the historical antecedents that shaped the emergence of Luperon High School during the 1990s in New York City. We documented the history of the school's formation based on oral history interviews with the founders. We also engaged in an historical review of the Dominican school system from which the majority of the students immigrated, using secondary sources and international assessments. Our goal was to understand why the founders of Luperon believed an additive approach to bilingual education would be better for Dominican students than the traditional 'subtractive' approach whereby learning English, not developing English and Spanish literacy, was the norm. Thus, we also examined the ways in which the federal No Child Left Behind policy, New York State accountability measures, and New York City's educational reforms under Mayor Michael Bloomberg impeded the efforts of Luperon but also afforded certain unusual 'work-arounds' and created a great degree of solidarity among school staff, parents, and students.

Second, in order to understand better how students' trajectories were mediated by counterproductive educational policies, post-secondary schooling, and the broader ethno-racially stratified economy, we decided to organize a longitudinal study of twenty newcomer immigrant youth. Our stratified sample included equal numbers of males and females and equal numbers of students from three categories of performance in their ESL (English as a Second Language) class: low, middle, and high based on a variety of English literacy tasks.

This element of the study involved annual interviews with this cohort of students over a period of four and a half years, beginning while they were in high school and followed by an interview four years after most had graduated high school. Four of these 20 students dropped out of high school: two because of pregnancy, and two because of failure on standardized tests. These four were among the most impoverished in the study. Four other students graduated and sought work immediately, but they found only service or retail positions that paid little more than they might have earned without a diploma. Eight members of the cohort went to community colleges; however, none had completed a degree four years later. The four remaining youth went to a four-year college upon graduating from Luperon High School. Yet, of these students, only one had graduated four years later. These outcomes give pause, indicating how additive bilingual education at a relatively successful high school is still conditioned by the "subtractive times" in which first-generation college students find themselves. If we had not studied the longer-term trajectories of these students beyond graduation, we might have assumed that the eight who had attended college or university had 'made it' and were succeeding in post-secondary education.

The benefit of a multi-year qualitative study is that it allowed us to extend the transversal axis, starting from the origins of Luperon and the conditions in Dominican and U.S. schools that necessitated an additive approach to bilingual education to four years after the focal cohort of students graduated from high school. Although it is rarely possible to carry out such an extended study as a graduate student, we encourage you to think about how a master's thesis or doctoral dissertation might be the starting point for a project that continues over time.

Exercise 5.2 How Might You Design a Longitudinal Qualitative Study?

Lesley Bartlett and Ofelia García conducted a longitudinal qualitative study of a bilingual high school for newcomer Dominican youth in New York City. To illuminate the transversal axis of additive bilingual education, they considered the history of the school's formation, and they examined policies related to education in the Dominican Republic and in the U.S. before and during the period under study that bear on migration patterns and the likelihood of graduation. One major strand of the study involved following the lives of twenty students at Luperon over a period of four and a half years, with another brief interview four years later, to see how the former students' trajectories were mediated by counter-productive educational policies, post-secondary schooling opportunities, and the broader ethno-racially stratified economy in both the U.S. and the Dominican Republic. By looking at change over time and space, the authors were able develop a comprehensive picture of how social mobility is limited even for graduates of a high school with a strong additive bilingual program.

As you reflect on this study, the following questions are intended to prompt you to think about how your own project might benefit from a temporal component.

It might involve the use of interviews, observations, and document analysis in one or more sites, or you might want to imagine your current project as the beginning of a study that might unfold (or could be revisited) over time:

- If you were to include *longitudinal interviews* with the same group(s) of people over time, who might be the people to track over time, and why? What might be the appropriate period of time to follow this group, and what is your rationale for doing so? How frequently might you wish to interview the participants? What topics might you want to discuss with them and why?
- Do you know of any 'restudies' in your field? If so, review them and identify the aspects of the restudy that you thought were successful? What might you change if you were to conduct the restudy and why?
- Are there any existing studies in your field that you think merit a restudy? If so, is a restudy feasible, and what would it require?
- If you were to plan your study so that the research you conduct now were to constitute the first phase, and you were to return to the site(s) and participant(s) at a later date for a restudy, what methods or questions would you need to include now to facilitate that possibility?

Example 5.2: Tracing the Transversal in a Mixed Methods Longitudinal Study of Secondary Schooling on Mount Kilimanjaro in Tanzania

Lesley Bartlett and Ofelia García's longitudinal study relied primarily on qualitative methods, but there are times when a combination of qualitative and quantitative methods may be most appropriate for a comparative case study. We have already discussed how a survey might include both closed and open-ended questions, and we have seen that it is possible to design the first phase of a study with the aim of returning to the same community and participants at a later date. Frances Vavrus has done just that in her research during the past 20 years that has explored various dimensions of secondary schooling in Old Moshi, a community of approximately 20,000 people in northern Tanzania (1996, 2003a, 2003b, 2015; Vavrus & Moshi, 2009). I (Frances) began working in Old Moshi as a secondary school teacher in 1993 and returned in 1996 as a doctoral student carrying out an ethnography of the school where I had taught three years earlier. Although I was not engaged in formal research the first time I lived in Old Moshi, the experience raised many questions about why secondary schooling for girls was so actively encouraged in this part of the country when international discourses generally characterized African parents as unsupportive of their daughters' education. I also wondered about the subtle differences in resources I noticed from one ridge of this mountainous community to another, such as more cinderblock houses around some of the primary schools in Old Moshi and electricity lines along one of the major dirt roads but not the other.

Over the course of the past two decades, I have carried out two longitudinal studies using mixed methods approaches. The first was based on research

I carried out for my dissertation in 1996, which I extended by conducting a follow-up survey and focus group discussions in 2000 with some of the same youth to explore how the desire for secondary schooling was contributing to the spread of HIV/AIDS (Vavrus, 2003a, 2003b). The second was a 12-year study of youth who had completed primary school in 2000 or 2001 in one of four different topographical zones in Old Moshi and whose post-primary trajectories included secondary schooling, vocational education, informal training, or no additional education at all (Vavrus, 2015; Vavrus & Moshi, 2009). In these two studies and others over the years, I have relied on five research methods to varying degrees: archival research, focus group discussions, interviewing, participant observation, and surveying. Focus groups, interviews, and participant observation have been discussed in other extended examples in this book, so I will limit my discussion in this section to archival research and surveys as potentially useful methods for studying the transversal axis of a comparative case study.

I carried out archival research in 1996 as part of my doctoral work, and it involved spending a month at the Tanzania National Archives in Dar es Salaam going through files containing correspondence, policies, and reports written by British colonial officials responsible for education and health in Tanganyika (as the mainland was called until 1964), and by Tanganyikan leaders—primarily chiefs and their scribes—in response to these policies. I was specifically seeking information about the Kilimanjaro Region and the chiefdom of Old Moshi to understand how contemporary attitudes towards schooling, especially for girls, and the current over-representation of post-primary schools in the area relative to the rest of rural Tanzania came to be. I also visited the major public hospital in the country at the time, Muhimbili Hospital, and the flagship national university, the University of Dar es Salaam, to locate reports, theses, and dissertations in their archives pertaining to girls' education and health. I have returned to these archival sources on many occasions over the years as I consider new perspectives on linkages between present and past.

The longitudinal survey project began in 2000, when I was a post-doctoral fellow, and it involved a research team comprised of four to five Tanzanian researchers for each round of data collection[6]. We developed surveys that were administered to 277 students who, in 2000, were in the final two years of primary school at one of four primary schools in Old Moshi (there were 11 primary schools at the time). We also administered a comprehensive household survey to each student's parent or guardian. These surveys were administered to all households in 2000, 2001, 2006, and 2012. The survey for the students was only administered in 2000, but we followed up with interviews of 36 of these former students in 2006–2007 and 20 of the 36 youth in 2012. These youth were selected for interviews based on the five post-primary school trajectories we had identified from the 2000 survey to ensure that we had representatives of each possible path: (1) immediate transition to secondary school; (2) delayed transition to secondary school; (3) enrollment in vocational or other formal educational programs; (4) informal or no training but employed; or (5) not employed or irregularly employed. Due to time and financial constraints, we selected interview participants who, in 2007 and 2012, were living in one of three regions of the country where my research assistant and I could travel relatively easily.

The student surveys in 2000 were primarily forward-looking, asking the youth both closed and open-ended questions about what they would like to be doing the following year, what level of education they sought, and what kind of jobs they hoped to have. The household surveys, on the other hand, asked almost exclusively closed questions about the educational histories of family members, including the highest level of education of the interviewee (typically a parent but sometimes a grandparent) and of the interviewee's spouse, parents, and other children. These surveys also asked about household wealth, such as electricity and water in the home, owning a bicycle or car, and land ownership for substance and cash crops; birth and death histories; and questions about aspirations for the student in the study (Vavrus, 2003a; 2015). Each time the survey was administered after 2001, we added a few open-ended questions regarding an issue of interest that had emerged as potentially relevant in explaining the differentiation over time in terms of the percentage of students, siblings, and parents from the four primary schools who had gone to secondary school or college. For example, we added questions about access to different sources of water in the 2001 survey because the initial survey in 2000 indicated that this might be a factor affecting girls' enrollment. We also added questions to subsequent surveys about new education policies that went into effect between 2002 and 2009, allowing us to integrate the analysis of quantitative data about education, births/deaths, and wealth with qualitative responses to these additional questions.

As in the Bartlett and García study, the advantage of following a cohort of youth over time meant that we were able to see how patterns of post-primary schooling were affected by topographic differences in the landscape of Old Moshi that likely influenced where missionaries and colonial officials established schools, clinics, and administrative outposts (Vavrus, 2015). For instance, among the 277 youth in the study, only 62 (22 percent) ended up going to secondary school in the year immediately following the completion of primary school and finishing the secondary school cycle six years later. Of the youth who did follow this path, those from the primary school catchment area nearest to the one paved road in the area were 3.4 times more likely than students from the other three catchment areas to have done so. Moreover, youth from the primary school located very close to one of the oldest secondary schools in the country were 3.11 times more likely than students from the other primary school catchment areas to have reached the level of college or university by 2012 (Vavrus, 2015). Coupling these quantitative findings from the survey with the archival research into when and where schools and other social institutions were established in Old Moshi allowed me to develop a theory regarding the social production of educational inequality over time and a framework for a critical geography of schooling.

Exercise 5.3 How Might You Integrate Archival and/or Survey Research in a Comparative Case Study?

Researchers typically do not bring archival and survey research together in the same project because archival research is seen as the domain of historians and interpretivist social scientists, and survey research is frequently used by positivist or post-positivist researchers who seek to find 'real' answers to the questions they ask. However, the research by Vavrus over the past two decades shows that the two methods can be used together productively when one's project warrants it. It may be most useful to you at this point to contemplate doing one or the other for your current project but to continue thinking about a master's thesis or a dissertation as the starting point for much longer engagement with a group of people, a place, or a core institution.

- If you wanted to explore the historical antecedents of the phenomenon of interest to you, what records might exist that trace its formation? You might think about policies, laws, minutes of meetings, letters, or other forms of correspondence. How could you go about locating archives where these materials might be kept?
- What systems have you developed so far to keep track of sources you have found for your study? Where could you learn about more exacting or robust ways of documenting what you are finding and ensuring that you can find specific information again when you need it?
- What aspects of your project might lend themselves to a survey as a way to learn more about the central phenomenon in the present and past? If you have not taken a class in survey design and analysis, is this a commitment you want to make and, if so, is it feasible to do so? If not, are there other resources at your university or in your network of colleagues that could help you plan, design, and/or analyze a survey?
- In what ways might a survey help you to illuminate the transversal axis of your comparative case study, if at all? How would it fit with the other methods of research you have planned?

Conclusion

In this chapter, we have laid out a rationale for the temporal dimension of the CCS approach and discussed a variety of methods that can be used to examine change over time in the phenomenon of interest to you. We also illustrated how different researchers, including ourselves, have used different combinations of these methods in their longitudinal studies and why the studies are stronger because of this temporal focus.

The importance of the transversal axis in the CCS approach cannot be overstated because it helps us as researchers redress the tendency to study social problems in the present with little analytical appreciation for the conditions that created them. It also reminds us to think about time and space as inextricably interconnected. Throughout this book, we have attempted to illustrate this point by showing how contemporary problems at the local or national level are rarely the result of spontaneous circumstances happening in 'the now' or circumscribed conditions that only affect one neighborhood, city, or state. There is a process to their manifestation that arises over time and in relation to decisions being made hundreds or thousands of miles away. Other scholars have argued for the importance of multi-sited and multi-scalar social research, and we could not agree more. To this call we add a temporal one to encourage the development of horizontal, vertical, and transversal axes.

Notes

1 We offer these examples even though we realize that graduate students, and many fellow professors, do not have multiple years to put into a single study. However, when we began these projects—Bartlett with the New York City study and Vavrus in the Kilimanjaro Region of Tanzania—we did not anticipate they would extend for as many years as they did.
2 This explanation is informed by two important sources. The first is a 1998 essay by Peter Stearns titled "Why Study History?" (available at https://www.historians.org/about-aha-and-membership/aha-history-and-archives/archives/why-study-history-%281998%29). The second is the introduction to *Knowing, Teaching, and Learning History* (Stearns, Seixas, & Wineburg, 2000).
3 See Crapanzano (1977, 1984) on the use of life history in the field of anthropology.
4 Readers with specific interests in education may wish to review some of the powerful U.S. histories of education that feature oral history techniques. Scholars like R. Scott Baker (2006), David Cecelski (1994), and Ansley Erickson (2016) have memorably engaged oral history to demonstrate how educational policies, including the closure of traditionally African American schools and the development of new curricula and testing policies, have reinforced racial inequalities throughout the American South.
5 Researchers on this project included César Fernández, Ali Michael, Jill Koyama, Norma Andrade, Elizabeth "Betsy" Cromwell Kim, Dina López, Carmina Makar, Ivana Espinet, and Natalie Catasús.
6 There were three members of the research team who participated in every round of data collection: Charles Moshi (team leader), Bertha Moshi, and Fideles Mero. Others who assisted with one or more rounds of surveying were Flora Kisaka, Edna Mero, and Frank Nyange. Emmanuel Moshi and Goodiel Moshi both contributed to data entry and analysis, and Zaina Mshana and Charles Moshi assisted with the interpretation of the qualitative and quantitative data throughout the life of the project.

References

Anderson, N. (1923). *The hobo*. Chicago: University of Chicago Press.
Baker, R. S. (2006). *Paradoxes of desegregation: African-American struggles for educational equity in Charleston, South Carolina, 1926–1972*. Columbia: University of South Carolina Press.
Bartlett, L., & García, O. (2011). *Additive schooling in subtractive times: Bilingual education and Dominican immigrant youth in the Heights*. Nashville, TN: Vanderbilt University Press.

Behar, R. (2003). *Translated woman: Crossing the border with Esperanza's story* (2nd ed.). Boston: Beacon Press.

Burton, L., Purvin, D., & Garrett-Peters, R. (2009). Longitudinal ethnography: Uncovering abuse in low-income women's lives. In G. H. Elder & J. Z. Giele (Eds.), *The craft of life course research* (pp. 70–92). New York: Guilford Press.

Cave, M., & Sloan, S. (2014). *Listening on the edge: Oral history in the aftermath of crisis.* New York: Oxford University Press.

Claus, P., & Marriot, J. (2012). *History: An introduction to theory, method and practice.* New York: Routledge.

Compton-Lilly, C. (2003). *Reading families: The literate lives of urban children.* New York: Teachers College Press.

Compton-Lilly, C. (2007). *Re-reading families: The literate lives of urban children, four years later.* New York: Teachers College Press.

Compton-Lilly, C. (2012). *Reading time: The literate lives of urban secondary school students and their families.* New York: Teachers College Press.

Compton-Lilly, C. (2015). Longitudinal studies and literacy studies. In J. Rowsell & K. Pahl (Eds.), *Routledge handbook for literacy studies* (pp. 218–210). New York: Routledge.

Cornwell, C., & Sutherland, E. (1937). *The professional thief.* Chicago: University of Chicago Press.

Crapanzano, V. (1977). The life history in anthropological fieldwork. *Anthropology and Humanism Quarterly 2,* 3–7.

Crapanzano, V. (1984). Life histories. *American Anthropologist 86*(4), 953–960.

Davis, K. (2007). *The making of Our Bodies, Ourselves: How feminism travels across borders.* Durham, NC: Duke University Press.

Demerath, P. (2009). *Producing success: The culture of personal advancement in an American high school.* Chicago: University of Chicago Press.

Demerath, P., Lynch, J., Milner, H. R., Peters, A., & Davidson, M. (2010). Decoding success: A middle-class logic of individual advancement in a U.S. suburb and high school. *Teachers College Record 112*(12), 2935–2987.

Derrida, J., & Prenowitz, E. (1995). Archive fever: A Freudian impression. *Diacritics 25*(2), 9–63.

Dodge, B. (2006). Re-imag(in)ing the past. *Rethinking History 10*(3), 347–367.

Domanska, E. (2008). A conversation with Hayden White. *Rethinking History 12*(1), 3–21.

Fowler, F. (2013). *Survey research methods* (5th ed.). Thousand Oaks, CA: Sage.

Frank, G. (1979). Finding the common denominator: A phenomenological critique of life history method. *Ethos 7*(1), 68–94.

Frank, G. (1995). Anthropology and individual lives: The story of the life history and the history of the life story. *American Anthropologist 97*(1), 145–148.

Gandhi, L. (1998). *Postcolonial theory: A critical introduction.* New York: Columbia University Press.

Glueck, S., & Glueck, E. (1950). *Unravelling juvenile delinquency.* Cambridge, MA: Harvard University Press.

Goodson, I. (2001). The story of life history: Origins of the life history method in sociology. *Identity 1*(2), 129–142.

Groves, R. M., Fowler, F. J., Couper, M. P., Lepkowski, J. M., Singer, E., & Tourangeau, R. (2009). *Survey methodology* (2nd ed.). New York: Wiley.

Hansen, J. (2010). The logic of qualitative survey research and its position in the field of social research methods. *Qualitative Social Research 11*(2). Retrieved from http://www.qualitative-research.net/index.php/fqs/article/view/1450/2946.

Holland, J. (2007). *Qualitative longitudinal research: Exploring ways of researching lives through time.* Real Life Methods Node of the ESRC National Centre for Research Methods Workshop held at London South Bank University. Retrieved from http://citeseerx.ist.psu.edu/viewdoc/download?doi=10.1.1.485.7802&rep=rep1&type=pdf.

Holland, J., Thomson, R., & Henderson, S. (2006). *Qualitative longitudinal research: A discussion paper*, Working Paper No. 21, Families & Social Capital ESRC Research Group, London South Bank University. Retrieved from http://www.lsbu.ac.uk/ahs/downloads/families/familieswp21.pdf.

Laub, J., & Sampson, R. (2003). *Shared beginnings, divergent lives: Delinquent boys to age 70.* Cambridge, MA: Harvard University Press.

Lewis, O. (1961). *The children of Sanchez: Autobiography of a Mexican family.* New York: Random House.

Linde, C. (1993). *Life stories: The creation of coherence.* New York: Oxford University Press.

Manoff, M. (2004). Theories of the archive from across the disciplines. *Portal: Libraries and the Academy 4*(1), 9–25. DOI: 10.1353/pla.2004.0015

Maynes, M. J., Pierce, J. L., & Laslett, B. (2012). *Telling stories: The use of personal narratives in the social sciences and history.* Ithaca, NY: Cornell University Press.

Munro, P. (1998). *Subject to fiction: Women teachers' life history narratives and the cultural politics of resistance.* Buckingham, UK: Open University Press.

Neale, B., & Flowerdew, J. (2003) Time, texture & childhood: The contours of longitudinal qualitative research. *International Journal of Social Research Methods 6*(3), 189–199.

Perks, R., & Thomson, A. (Eds.) (1998). *The oral history reader* (2nd ed.). New York: Routledge.

Portelli, A. (2003). *The order has been carried out: History, memory, and meaning of a Nazi massacre in Rome.* New York: Palgrave Macmillan.

Ramsey, A. E., Sharer, W. B., L'Eplattenier, W. B., & Mastrangelo, B. (Eds.) (2010). *Working in the archives: Practical research methods for rhetoric and composition.* Carbondale, IL: Southern Illinois University Press.

Ritchie, D. (2011). *The Oxford handbook of oral history.* New York: Oxford University Press.

Rosenwald, G. C., & Ochberg, R. L. (Eds.) (1992). *Storied lives: The cultural politics of self-understanding.* New Haven, CT: Yale University Press.

Saldaña, J. (2003). *Longitudinal qualitative research: Analyzing change through time.* Walnut Creek, CA: AltaMira Press.

Shaw, C. (1930). *The jack-roller.* Chicago: University of Chicago Press.

Sheftel, A., & Zembrzycki, S. (Ed.) (2013). *Oral history off the record: Toward an ethnography of practice.* New York: Palgrave.

Shostak, M. (1961). *Nisa: The life and words of a !Kung woman.* Cambridge, MA: Harvard University Press.

Stearns, P. (1998). *Why study history?* Retrieved from https://www.historians.org/about-aha-and-membership/aha-history-and-archives/archives/why-study-history-%281998%29.

Stearns, P., Seixas, P., & Wineburg, S. (Eds.) (2000). *Knowing, teaching, and learning history*. New York: New York University Press.

Vavrus, F. (1996). *Schooling, fertility, and the discourse of development: A study of the Kilimanjaro region of Tanzania* (unpublished doctoral dissertation). University of Wisconsin, Madison.

Vavrus, F. (2003a). *Desire and decline: Schooling amid crisis in Tanzania*. New York: Peter Lang.

Vavrus, F. (2003b). "The acquired income deficiency syndrome": School fees and sexual risk in northern Tanzania. *Compare* 33(2), 235–250.

Vavrus, F. (2015). Topographies of power: Critical historical geography in the study of education in Tanzania. *Comparative Education*. DOI: 10.1080/03050068. 2015.1112567

Vavrus, F., & Moshi, G. (2009). The cost of a "free" primary education in Tanzania. *International Journal of Educational Policy, Research, and Practice* 8, 31–42.

Weis, L. (1990). *Working class without work*. New York: Routledge.

Weis, L. (2004). *Class reunion: The remaking of the American white working class*. New York: Routledge.

Yin, R. K. (2014). *Case study research: Design and methods* (5th ed.). Thousand Oaks, CA: Sage.

6 Follow the Inquiry

Reflections on Comparative Case Study Research

We hope the heuristic of horizontal, vertical, and transversal axes in the CCS approach has proven to be fruitful to you in thinking about your current or future research. While single case studies can be useful, we wanted you to consider the value of building into your study a comparative approach. You may have decided, definitively, that this approach does not match your epistemological orientation, your methodological preparation, or your available temporal and monetary resources. That, too, is a worthwhile discovery—in being explicit, methodologically, about what we *don't* want to do and *why*, we can gain greater clarity about our goals, purposes, and plans.

Our original impetus in developing this approach stemmed from our efforts to explain to colleagues in comparative social science fields the value and virtues of qualitative, and even ethnographic, research methods. We hoped to increase the space in the field of comparative education, in particular, for work that is decidedly qualitative, though not necessarily exclusively so. An important additional goal, from the start, has been to encourage qualitative researchers to think more creatively and broadly about research possibilities, including the study of policy. Too often, qualitative researchers select an issue, a community, or a population as their case, and then burrow deep into the topic, collecting rich, compelling, and 'thick' data but sometimes without situating this case within a wider landscape of relevant issues, factors, or trends. We, too, have been guilty of conducting research that did not sufficiently account for how the enduring dilemma(s) or phenomena that were the focus of our studies might have varied across groups or sites. This book has been our effort to share what we have learned over the years about case study research and the importance of comparison across space, scales, and time.

At a minimum, we hope to convince researchers such as yourself of the value of including in a research project what we might call a 'broadening' phase. For example, a study on the challenges faced by newcomer Latino youth in secondary schools in a specific 'new Latino destination' city in the U.S. southeast could begin by conducting key informant interviews with principals and educators at all ten high schools in the district before selecting one or more focal schools. A project on one country's policies to promote civic engagement among youth could be expanded to compare these policies to recommendations and initiatives of international development institutions and/or to the enactment of those policies in the everyday life of a civic engagement program. A study of identity formation among a group of political activists might explore how the conditions that have given rise to their protests came into being over the course of years, decades, or longer spans of time. We can imagine doing such 'broadening' work at the beginning of the study, which would help not only with research design but also with case selection, or near the conclusion of the study, when insights derived from the primary study could be examined in the light of other cases.[1]

Related to this call, we encourage scholars who primarily use qualitative methods to be both more *daring* and more *explicit* in their methodological decisions. The advent of multi-sited ethnographic work, network ethnography, methods influenced by actor network theory, and similar approaches provides scholars with substantial methodological flexibility to entertain the possibility of conducting studies that focus on more than one school, group, or community. This is not to say that there isn't still much to be learned from a small, focused ethnographic study; rather, we believe this should not be the default option for a qualitative researcher. Terms like "ethnography" or "case study" have served as a kind of methodological blanket in two senses—first, they have offered the comforting sense that we are continuing in a revered line of research, but, second, they have shielded us from the necessity of explaining, quite explicitly, our methodological choices. There are times when even we, diehard fans of ethnography, feel like ethnographers demand that we suspend our disbelief and trust in the veracity or value of their story. This makes it very difficult for novice researchers to understand how one goes about conducting such research, and it frequently leads to less convincing or compelling analyses.

We believe that new kinds of studies are needed that inventively defy traditional expectations of thick description for only one locale while minimizing or outright ignoring the forces by which this case was constituted. We suggest following a process or phenomenon across space and time, such as when Desmond (2016) followed the processes of eviction as he moved through trailer parks, public housing units, eviction courts, shelters, abandoned houses, churches, funerals, and AA meetings in a single city, documenting poverty as a relationship. At the same time, we need these methods of tracing ideologies, processes, and policies to be explicit. We need to explain, in our work, the logic of our methodological decisions. Perhaps we avoid this kind of talk because it feels imitative of quantitative sampling approaches, but we have found that explicitly accounting for the choices we make in terms of selecting cases, sites, populations, events, and techniques makes for much more substantial research.

Another impetus for this book, as more thoroughly described in Chapter 2, is to breathe new perspectives into the case study literature itself. For many years, we have taught research methods courses and felt that the available and widely circulating literature on case studies is, simply, wanting. Let's reconsider, for a moment, Yin's definition of a case study as inquiry that "investigates a contemporary phenomenon ('the case') in depth and within its real-world context, especially when the boundaries between phenomenon and context may not be clearly evident" (2014, p. 16). Why focus on the contemporary, divorced from the past? What does he mean by "real-world context"? If "phenomenon and the context" are not clearly bounded, why does much of the case study literature make 'bounding' the case such an important step in the research design? Too often context is presumed to signal place. It is important to expand our notion of context spatially and relationally. We have read passages from this literature on context and culture and felt them to be limited, limiting, and not well aligned with most contemporary interpretivist social science. We balk at the suggestion that case study research is primarily descriptive or exploratory, with little explanatory or analytical power. Moreover, we think there is immense, untapped potential in comparative cases of the type that we have described here, which go well beyond the "replication logic" suggested by Yin (2014) or the acontextual vision of comparison that echoes through Stake (1995). Students in too many fields are introduced to a very limited conceptualization of qualitative case studies and of their analytical and theoretical potential. We hope this volume has made some progress toward expanding the possibilities of case study research.

Frequently Asked Questions

When presenting our work on comparative case studies, we frequently encounter similar questions from people who are interested in, or even cautiously enthusiastic about, the CCS approach, but who are not yet certain that it is right for their work. In this section, we address some of these questions in the hopes that they will allay concerns.

What Is a Case?

This seems like a straightforward question, does it not? Except it isn't. It's a very tricky one, as we discussed in Chapter 2. Let's say you want to study learner-centered pedagogy, and you identify six Tanzanian secondary schools as homologous horizontal cases (as we and our colleagues did—see Chapter 1). Are the schools your cases? Are the participating teachers in the schools your cases? Is phenomenon of the learner-centered pedagogy, as promoted by development organizations and implemented by the Tanzanian government, your case?

Cases are traditionally denoted, from the beginning of the study, with time and place boundaries—e.g., New York's Chinatown from 1990 to 2000, or Mr. Adam's classroom in Central Elementary School in Chicago in 2016. But throughout the book we have argued against the impulse to rigidly 'bound' the study *a priori*. We aver that traditional notions of context, which are often place-specific, should be enhanced by attention to "fuzzy fields," as well as by structures and processes beyond the specific place of study that help to socially produce that place and relations within it. In other words, we promote a notion of context that is informed by the concept of social field (à la Bourdieu) and by spatial theory, rather than a place-bound concept. In addition, we have cautioned against the tendency to denote, deductively and before the initiation of the study, a time period, as it often causes us to focus on the present and might lead us to ignore events that fall outside this temporal delineation, even if these events are revealed through the research process to be significant. Instead, we encourage scholars to *follow the inquiry* and allow the study to unfold, depending on where the data lead. This fundamental move honors the commitment of qualitative scholarship to include inductive reasoning (often by combining it with deductive reasoning). As anthropologist John Comaroff said about ethnography, this work

> rests on a *dialectic between the deductive and the inductive*, between the concept and the concrete, between its objectives and its subjects, *whose intentions and inventions frequently set its agendas*. The failure to grasp this may account in part for the autonomic dismissal of ethnography as unrigorous, unreplicable, [and] unfalsifiable.
>
> (As quoted in Becker, 2009, p. 546, emphasis ours)

Thus, scholars who wish to define cases as empirical units must, when using the CCS approach, constantly revisit the bounds or delimitations of their case. In addition, it is valuable to consider that empirical sampling may be people-focused (e.g., families or on-line communities), structure-focused (e.g. organizations), or activity-focused (e.g., critical incidents) (Patton, 2002). Each of these approaches requires us to rethink the notion of context.

Another approach to defining a case or cases is to waive an empirical definition of cases in favor of a theoretical one (Ragin, 1992). In this view, cases are not *found* but *made*—they result from our theoretical constructs. Thus, a scholar may be interested in the concept of state fragility and therefore use this concept to 'make' a comparative study of Somalia and South Sudan; or a scholar may be interested in the phenomenon of alternative cultural capital formation among high-school-aged youth and use that concept to 'make' cases from two arts programs in Chicago. Further, these cases may only become apparent over time, as the data collection and analysis unfold. In such a situation, like Ragin and Becker, we urge researchers to continually ask: "What is this a case of?" In considering that question:

> The less sure that researchers are of their answers, the better their research may be. From this perspective, no definitive answer to the question "What is a case?" can or should be given, especially not at the outset, because *it depends*. The question should be asked again and again, and researchers should treat any answer to the question as tentative and specific to the evidence and issues at hand. Working through the relations of ideas to evidence answers the question "What is this a case of?"
>
> (Ragin, 1992, p. 6)

Thus, scholars have to think about whether they are using an empirical notion of a case or a theoretical notion of a case, and whether they embrace an *a priori* or evolving delimitation of the case. To complicate matters further, some combination of these could be mobilized—one might begin with an empirical notion of a case but allow it to remain flexible over time, resulting in a more theoretical definition. Thus, as we can see, the question "What is a case?" is quite complex, indeed.

Exercise 6.1 What Are Your Cases?

As described above, cases can be defined in a number of ways.

- What are the different possible ways in which you could define the case or cases in your study?
- What are the implications of each choice in terms of methodological techniques, time, money, and/or speaking to a specific audience with your work?

How Do I Select Cases?

It is essential to recognize that your definition of a case and your overall episte-mological stance will shape your strategy for selecting cases. As we discussed in the first two chapters, case studies that are oriented by what Maxwell (2013) calls a variance approach generally aim for a form of generalizability that aligns with a neo-positivist epistemology. That is to say, they often implic-itly accept the idea that case studies should elucidate features of a broader population. Common strategies for case selection, given this stance, include typical, diverse, extreme, deviant, influential, most different, and most similar approaches (Seawright & Gerring, 2008; see also Patton, 2002). Alternately, researchers guided by an interpretivist orientation may choose cases for their intrinsic qualities (Stake, 1995). In other words, the case is often selected for its own sake, because the context is inherently of interest to the researcher.

In contrast, process-oriented studies generally use an emergent design, fol-lowing the inquiry as it evolves across the lifespan of the research. Given the argument above regarding how cases may be made and not found, we suggest that you routinely ask yourself whether you are looking at the best case or cases to help you understand the phenomenon at the core of your study as your research progresses.

In general, qualitative case studies, whether following the CCS approach or not, do not aspire to statistical generalizability; they aim for analytical generalization through theory. Process-oriented studies seek to generate such insights. They tend to use a form of purposive sampling in case selection, but with the caveat that sampling may be an emergent process. Purposive sam-pling seeks to select cases that are relevant to the conceptual framework and the research questions, generate rich data on the phenomenon of interest, enhance the analytical generalizability, or transfer of insights, from the study, and produce believable, trustworthy descriptions and explanations (Miles & Huberman, 1994). As Patton (2002) noted, there are a range of specific strategies for purposive, or what he calls purposeful, case selection. They include (and here we are paraphrasing, but staying quite close to his words):

- *Extreme cases:* Learning from highly unusual manifestations of the phenomenon of interest, such as outstanding successes or notable failures, crises, etc.
- *Typical cases:* Selecting populations or events considered typical, normal, or average for a particular phenomenon. For example, instead of observing a classroom daily for 30 days, one might choose to observe that class on what the principal or teacher determines to be a typical day.
- *Intense cases:* Include information-rich cases that manifest the phenomenon intensely (not extremely), as in below-average students rather than the lowest- or highest-performing students.
- *Maximum variation of cases:* Purposefully picking a wide range of variation on a dimension or several dimensions of interest. This strategy could document variations that emerge in adapting to different conditions. It also identifies important common patterns that cut across variations. For example, if you are interested in how first (or home) language affects high-school achievement, you would want to identify all the present language groups in a school and be sure to include multiple participants from each group.
- *Homogeneous cases:* Selecting cases that minimize variation. This strategy simplifies analysis. In the example provided above, a study might focus only on students whose first language is Spanish.
- *Politically-important cases:* Such cases attract attention to the study (or you could avoid attracting undesired attention by purposefully eliminating from the sample politically-sensitive cases).
- *Criterion-based cases:* Cases that meet some predetermined criterion or criteria of importance. For example, someone studying how new voter registration laws influence political participation might interview all those who were not allowed to vote at select polling sites. The sites themselves might be selected using different criteria, such as socio-economic status of surrounding homes.
- *Convenient cases:* Selecting a case or cases for their convenience; thus, this is technically not purposeful. It saves time, money, and effort, but provides a poor rationale and low credibility for findings.
- *Critical cases:* Cases that are likely to "yield the most information and have the greatest impact on the development of knowledge" (Patton, 2002, p. 236).
- *Theory-based or operational construct cases:* When scholars seek manifestations of a theoretical construct of interest so as to elaborate and examine the construct (Patton, 2002, pp. 231–241).

Patton, and other authors, provide strategies beyond those listed above that may be more appropriate for your study (e.g., Palys, 2008; Becker, 1998). For example, you may prefer a most-similar design, which looks for cases with the presence of many similar causal factors but the absence of the outcome of interest, or a most-different design, which compares cases that vary by the presence of potentially causal factors but nonetheless share the outcome (or dependent, structures, organizations, activities, or variable) of interest (e.g., Przeworksi & Teune, 1982). The point is that you need to think critically about the people, places, events, partnerships, and/or theoretical constructs you are sampling, and why—and you need to be able to *explain those to yourself and your audience*.

Furthermore, and this is crucial to note, *you may use different sampling strategies, or logics, for different parts of your study*. For example, imagine that your phenomenon of interest is nurse–patient interactions in end-of-life care. You might select a *typical* hospice program at a hospital; stratify the nurse participants by some criterion you expect to be important, such as years of experience; and use *maximum variation* sampling to select the communication incidents will you observe. Once you have completed that phase of the work, you might 'broaden' the study by comparing this hospice program to one where nurses and patients typically share the same religious faith or ethnicity. If you have developed from the first phase a theory regarding a key factor that influences communication, you might identify a case featuring the same factor and see if you find the same outcomes. Alternately, if you adopt a process orientation, you may originally select three cases to study a phenomenon, but after an initial round of data collection, you may realize you need to add another site (or more), consistent with purposeful logic, for reasons that become clear as you do the work.

It is important that you not fall back on neo-positivist considerations to guide case selection if you are pursuing a process orientation. As Small (2009) reported in his ingenious article, "'How Many Cases Do I Need?': On Science and the Logic of Case Selection in Field-Based Research," new scholars are often urged to select cases using the goal of statistical generalization and the language of logical positivism, when neither match their aims. They are encouraged to make their samples representative or unbiased, imposing a language and logic that do not fit their goals. Small suggested, instead, that logical inference, informed by the discovery of relationships, should inform case selection and the effort to transfer insights. He explained:

> It would be erroneous for [someone] to hypothesize that because he observed a preponderance of, say, public cocaine consumption in his neighborhood, then the average poor neighborhood will exhibit a preponderance of cocaine use in public. In this hypothesis, logic played no role; it is a descriptive inference based on one case .... But suppose [the researcher] had observed that whenever a crime erupted in the neighborhood, some people retreated into their homes while others felt compelled to get organized. He also observed that those in the

latter group had stronger connections to the neighborhood … [He] might have uncovered a causal relationship between attachment and participation. He might then hypothesize that the reaction to crime will depend on the strength of local attachment, such that those strongly attached (through various mechanisms) are likely to participate while those weakly attached are likely to retreat. This is not a descriptive hypothesis; it is a logical … one.

(pp. 22–23)

Thus, Small urged scholars to move away from a naïve effort to generalize, statistically, from a case. Instead, he posited that a single case can generate valuable propositions regarding processes, which can be examined in other cases.[2]

Overall, we exhort qualitative researchers to be more transparent about the logic of their methodological choices. We have known many qualitative researchers who avoid a discussion of methods, as if thinking explicitly about research methods will automatically ally them with a neo-positivist orientation. We have read many ethnographies that fail to give an account of research methods; we've heard talks that forgo all discussion of research strategies; and we've heard qualitative colleagues claim that any effort to compare flattens and thus diminishes the cases under consideration. We feel strongly that an unwillingness to discuss methods has undermined the possibilities for qualitative research to have a greater impact on policy and public debates because, essentially, we are asking audiences to trust our methods rather than explaining their logic.

Exercise 6.2 Case Selection

Case selection in a process-oriented study presents challenges if you are seeking to follow the inquiry and not 'bound' the case or cases at the outset. If you think about your study as consisting of phases with case selection being more emergent, you might want to consider these questions as you are designing your study and throughout the research process:

- What different case selection strategies or logics might you use for different phases of your study? What are the pros and cons of each strategy?
- What logistical challenges, such as getting research permission from your university's human subjects oversight panel (often called an institutional review board or IRB), might these strategies impose that would be different from setting out your cases *a priori*?

When Is a Case Not a Case?

Here is another wrinkle: Part of your study may not be a case at all. Depending on how you conceptualize your study, you may have elements that don't fit as a 'case.' For example, if you were to conduct a comparative case study of corporate sponsorship of girls' education programs in Rwanda, you might select two programs as your cases, or you might identify 20 young women (purposively sampled using select criteria) in one program, or across several programs, as your cases. You might then move across scales to do interviews with the corporate funder(s) based in Rwanda, South Africa, and Belgium. In such a scenario, you might conceptualize the research in the two programs or with the 20 young women as "cases" but the interviews at other scales as background or contextual information—and that's fine. Alternately, if you conceptualize your case as the phenomenon of girls' education programs in Africa sponsored by one corporation such as Nike, then the entire network of actors who get enrolled in planning and enacting Nike programs become part of your case. Notably, in this approach, the single case is inherently comparative. Your understanding of the case will evolve as you answer Ragin's question, "*What is this a case of?*"

In addition, given the emergent nature of qualitative research, you may add elements mid-stream that were not originally planned, or you may pursue some part of the work that ends up being irrelevant to the study at hand. There may be dead ends and U-turns during the research process that inform the work only indirectly as background information (or, sometimes, not at all). Although this can be frustrating when time and money for a study are limited, these moments should not be completely dismissed. You may revisit these experiences and find them to be sources of inspiration for future projects.

How Do I Analyze the Data?

Another question we are frequently asked concerns how to analyze the data of which a comparative case study is composed. Each CCS will require a different data analysis plan because each will be composed of different methods. In other words, there is no single way of analyzing data using the CCS approach because it encourages the use of multiple methods. It may seem obvious but is worth spelling out: If your study entails archival research, then follow the standards in history for analyzing archival materials; if it includes discourse analysis, then you will need specific training in how to analyze these data. The data analysis plan has to be tailored to include all of the methods used. If your study involves surveys or other methods requiring quantitative analysis, you will have to maintain quite different logics in the data analysis from those that drive the analysis of observations. In any situation, though, it is important not to allow the sometimes more familiar, and often more dominant, neo-positivist epistemology of one method to dictate the terms of data analysis for the others.

There are some data analysis techniques specific to comparison that you may find useful, providing you followed a sampling frame that is consistent with their logic. For example, Miles and Huberman (1994) discussed comparative case analysis. They recommended "stacking comparable cases" (p. 176), which entails writing a series of cases with an eye toward key factors shared across cases, and then using matrices or other display formats to compare across and explore interrelationships. Bazeley (2013) offered a nice illustration of this effort, aiming

> to explore similarities and differences across cases, with a view to increasing understanding of the processes that shape each case and the hope of identifying more general patterns and processes that can then assist in understanding experience or explaining behavior across a wider population.
>
> (p. 275)

Ragin (1997, 1993) developed a Boolean qualitative case analysis (QCA) technique to examine the various ways in which specified factors interact and combine with one another to yield particular outcomes. George and Bennett (2004) discussed process-tracing, which forces the researcher to consider alternative paths through which the outcome might have prevailed and then to compare with other examples to reveal the conditions under which given outcomes occur. Small (2009) outlined a sequential case analytical technique. All of these are feasible, provided they match your research design and case sampling strategy.

Keep in mind that qualitative data collected with a process orientation requires an emergent, iterative approach to analysis. This statement does not absolve us from having a data analysis plan. On the contrary, in some ways we need to be more explicit about our initial data analysis plan, our intention to remain flexible as data analysis unfolds, and the logic we expect to use to process our methodological decisions. Heath and Street (2008) encouraged qualitative researchers to review their data on a regular basis—e.g., weekly or monthly, depending on the intensity of data collection. They helpfully suggested that researchers write regular conceptual memos, which could include three sections: (1) "problems and setbacks ... [which] indicate unexpected occurrences"; (2) "overview, [which] indicates the hours in the field, physical locations, and primary sources of data"; and (3) "patterns, insights, and breakthroughs, [where] the ethnographer hones in on patterns detected, insights or trends, and 'aha!' realizations" (p. 80). Overall, it is important to provide a clear articulation of your conceptual and empirical goals and methodological decisions. Such statements make it easier for general readers and reviewers to evaluate the quality of the work.

Most importantly, your data analysis plan will require an extra step— a synthesis of the data collected across multiple sites, scales, times, and methods. The mixed methods literature discusses synthesis as a phase of the research and provides some guidance for this phase (e.g., Heyvaert, Maes, & Onghena, 2013; Small, 2013; Boaz et al., 2006). If different techniques are meant to answer the *same* question, scholars might pursue synthesis by aggregation, which "entails the assimilation of findings considered to address the same relationship or connection between two or more aspects of a target phenomenon" (Sandelowski, Voils, Leeman, & Crandell, 2012, p. 323). If different techniques are meant to answer distinct but related questions, scholars might pursue synthesis by configuration, which

> entails the arrangement of thematically diverse individual findings, or sets of aggregated findings, into a coherent theoretical rendering of them. In contrast to the judgment of thematic similarity among findings required to aggregate findings, findings in configuration syntheses are conceived as thematically diverse and therefore as not amenable to pooling. Instead of confirming each other (by virtue of repetition of what are judged to be the same aspects or associations), thematically diverse findings may contradict, extend, explain, or otherwise modify each other.
>
> (Sandelowski et al., 2012, p. 325)

Thus, configuration requires scholars to consider and resolve, analytically, the disparate and at times discrepant evidence provided via different methodological techniques. Though challenging, this approach can be extremely fruitful.

Exercise 6.3   How Will You Analyze Your Data?

Consider the different possibilities for data analysis outlined above and the different methods for conducting your study that you have written about in earlier chapters.

- Which approaches do you believe are more consistent with your research questions, methods, and case selection strategy? Imagine that you are writing this as a proposal for funding. What argument can you put forward to defend your views?
- Write a short paragraph or two in which you describe your data analysis plan for your most immediate audience, whether it is for a doctoral committee, funding review committee, or a general audience of readers in your field.

Isn't the CCS Approach Simply too Ambitious?

This may be the question we receive most frequently. For the most part, people seem unsettled by the emergent nature of the research. They wonder: "How can I plan the work? How can I anticipate how long I will be in the field? When will I know I have completed certain phases of research?" Such questions are understandable for many reasons. Scholars typically have to submit a plan for funding and for the IRB committee; some may need to schedule when research will be completed and publications submitted for promotion and tenure reviews; doctoral students may need to anticipate when they will complete the dissertation and graduate. To such concerns, we say: Yes, these are real concerns, but we know it is possible to use the CCS approach because we have done it, and we have advised many students, now colleagues, who have used it. The truth is, researchers who use multi-sited ethnography or participatory action research face many of the same challenges. Comparative case studies require intellectual dexterity and methodological flexibility; they demand a regular review of the data collected to date and an analysis of emergent findings while the research is underway (as opposed to waiting until data collection is completed); and they necessitate thinking of research as composed of phases so that one phase can inform methodological decisions for the next phase.

In part, though, the question is motivated not only by the uncertainty caused by emergent methods, but also by the anxiety generated when one thinks of trying to work across scales, or across methods, or across sites. One answer to this dilemma is to work in research teams, even when one is a doctoral student or faculty member required to produce a single-authored study. A team might focus on the same problematic, while members work on various parts of it. For example, members might divide into sub-teams dedicated to the horizontal, vertical, and transversal axes of a large project from which many studies emerge. However, as discussed by the Mixed Methods Working Group (Weis, Eisenhart, & Duncan, 2016), constituting a mixed methods team poses a challenge:

> Investigators tend to develop in-depth expertise in particular theoretical and methodological perspectives. Those who lead and become part of mixed methods and multi-disciplinary teams must exhibit an intellectual and personal flexibility. They must also see the value of other methods and perspectives and develop a willingness to work across these methods and perspectives in the service of broad-based research questions. .... The goal is not to undermine the value of one methodological or disciplinary perspective but rather to recognize that approaching questions from a mixed perspective has the potential to expand the knowledge base in key areas.
>
> (p. 4)

In all teams, whether mixed methods or not, it is essential to have regular team meetings to debrief, develop emergent propositions with adequate supporting evidence, and tweak the methodological techniques accordingly. This option is more feasible at certain stages of one's career than others, and it will depend heavily on the availability of funding or the willingness of researchers to essentially dedicate (and sometimes donate) their time to a collective effort. Further, there are challenges to team research; if you select this option, it may serve you well to read the available literature on this topic in the sociology of social research (e.g., Leahey, 2008). As we have learned from our own collaborative efforts, challenges may emerge in the areas of selection and mobility; funding; mentoring, training, and socialization; communication; timing; and the research process (Bartlett et al., 2013; see also Creese & Blackledge, 2012).

Another answer to the question of whether a comparative case study is too ambitious is to rely on secondary sources for one axis. For example, you could use primarily sources written by others for the transversal axis and focus your own energies on the horizontal and/or vertical axis. As we stated in Chapter 1, few of us can give equal attention to all three axes. Limitations of time and money will make it difficult for most researchers except those with a great deal of time and a research team to conduct equally rich analyses along each axis. Nonetheless, we aver that it can be valuable to consider all of the axes in designing the study, and to consider whether and how to add them more centrally at a later date.

Exercise 6.4 Considering Your Own Constraints

While in this book we argue against setting your case boundaries *a priori*, we are fully aware that researchers have limited time, money, and other resources to spend on research.

- What are your constraints, both professionally and personally?
- How might these constraints shape the study that you design?
- What strategies might you use to overcome some of them?

Conclusions

We wrote this book with many of our former and current students and colleagues in mind because we have been fortunate to watch as they have developed comparative case studies and to talk with them about how to refine the approach and our articulation of it. They have helped us generate the questions in this chapter and the exercises throughout the book, which came from years of teaching research methods courses and dissertation seminars.

We encourage you to consider the CCS approach for a current or future project, especially one that might otherwise be quite bounded culturally, spatially, or temporally. Whether you decide to do so or not, we hope the exercises in the book serve as a guide for any research journey upon which you might embark because they were designed to follow a process of thinking through a new project that many of us in the interpretive social sciences have found useful.

Final Note. We would love to hear from readers as they use the CCS approach. We can imagine how this approach could be applied in fields as varied as communication studies and rural sociology. We particularly seek examples in fields underrepresented in this volume. Further, we also welcome your questions and suggestions on how to make this book more useful to future researchers.

Notes

1 This decision is not unlike discussions in the mixed methods literature on the value of sequential, versus simultaneous, mixed methods work (e.g., Small, 2011; Teddlie & Tashakkori, 2008).
2 Further, Small (2009) drew on Yin (2002) and Ragin and Becker (1992) to recommend that qualitative researchers reject statistical "sampling logic" in favor of what he called inferential "case study logic." He explained that sampling logic refers to the idea that all units will have an equal probability of selection and will be subject to the same research procedures (e.g., questionnaire), thus producing statistical representativeness. He contrasted this approach to "case study logic," a version of Yin's replication model but with an important, sequential twist. Small suggested that case studies might proceed by following a sequence:

> In a case model, the number of units (cases) is unknown until the study is completed; the collection of units is, by design, not representative; each unit has its own probability of selection; and different units are subject to different questionnaires. The first unit or case yields a set of findings and a set of questions that inform the next case. If the study is conducted properly, the very last case examined will provide very little new or surprising information. The objective is saturation. An important component of case study design is that each subsequent case attempts to replicate the prior ones. Through 'literal replication' a similar case is found to determine whether the same mechanisms are in play; through 'theoretical replication' a case different according to the theory is found to determine whether the expected difference is found. Sampling logic is superior when asking descriptive questions about a population; case study logic is probably more effective when asking how or why questions about processes unknown before the start of the study.
>
> (pp. 24–25)

Small explained how a scholar could conduct a series of interviews as if each were a successive case, gathering more and more refined data about a proposition.

References

Bartlett, L., Bermeo, M. J., Boniface, T., Mogusu, E., Ngarina, D., Rugambwa, A., Salema, V., Thomas, M., Vavrus, F., & Webb, T. (2013). International collaboration: Processes, benefits, tensions, and conclusions. In F. Vavrus & L. Bartlett (Eds.), *Teaching in tension: International pedagogies, national policies, and teachers' practices in Tanzania* (pp. 169–194). Rotterdam: Sense Publishers.
Bazeley, P. (2013). *Qualitative data analysis: Practical strategies*. Thousand Oaks, CA: Sage.
Becker, H. S. (1998). *Tricks of the trade: How to think of your research while you are doing it*. Chicago: University of Chicago Press.

Becker, H. S. (2009). How to find out how to do qualitative research. *International Journal of Communication* 3, 545–553.

Boaz, A., Ashby, D., Denyer, D., Egan, M., Harden, A., Jones, D. R., Pawson, R., & Tranfield, D. (2006). A multitude of syntheses: A comparison of five approaches from diverse policy fields. *Evidence & Policy: A Journal of Research, Debate and Practice* 2(4), 479–502.

Creese, A., & Blackledge, A. (2012). Voice and meaning-making in team ethnography. *Anthropology & Education Quarterly* 43, 306–324.

Desmond, M. (2016). *Evicted: Poverty and profit in the American city*. New York: Crown.

George, A. L., & Bennett, A. (2004). *Case studies and theory development in the social sciences*. Cambridge, MA: MIT Press.

Heath, S. B., & Street, B. (2008). *On ethnography: Approaches to language and literacy research*. New York: Teachers College Press.

Heyvaert, M., Maes, B., & Onghena, P. (2013). Mixed methods research synthesis: Definition, framework, and potential. *Quality and Quantity* 47(2), 659–676.

Leahey, E. (2008). Methodological memes and mores: Toward a sociology of social research. *Annual Review of Sociology* 34, 33–53.

Maxwell, J. A. (2013). *Qualitative research design: An interactive approach* (3rd ed.). Thousand Oaks, CA: Sage.

Miles, M., & Huberman, A. (1994). *Qualitative data analysis*. London: Sage.

Palys, T. (2008). Purposive sampling. In L. M. Given (Ed.), *The Sage encyclopedia of qualitative research methods* (Vol. 2) (pp. 697–698). Los Angeles: Sage.

Patton, M. Q. (2002). *Qualitative research and evaluation methods*. Thousand Oaks, CA: Sage.

Przeworksi, A., & Teune, H. (1982). *The logic of comparative social inquiry*. Malabar: Krieger.

Ragin, C. (1992). Introduction: Cases of "What is a case?" In C. Ragin & H. Becker (Eds.), *What is a case? Exploring the foundations of social inquiry* (pp. 1–18). New York: Cambridge University Press.

Ragin, C. (1993). Introduction to qualitative comparative analysis. In T. Janoski & A. Hicks (Eds.), *The comparative political economy of the welfare state* (pp. 299–319). New York: Cambridge University Press.

Ragin, C. (1997). Turning the tables: How case-oriented research challenges variable-oriented research. *Comparative Social Research* 16, 27–42.

Ragin, C., & Becker, H. (1992). *What is a case? Exploring the foundations of social inquiry*. New York: Cambridge University Press.

Sandelowski, M., Voils, C., Leeman, J., & Crandell, J. (2012). Mapping the mixed methods–mixed research synthesis terrain. *Journal of Mixed Methods Research* 6(4), 317–331.

Seawright, J., & Gerring, J. (2008). Case selection techniques in case study research: A menu of qualitative and quantitative options. *Political Research Quarterly* 61, 294–308.

Small, M. L. (2009). "How many cases do I need?": On science and the logic of case selection in field-based research. *Ethnography* 10(1), 5–38.

Small, M. L. (2011). How to conduct a mixed-methods study: Trends in a rapidly growing literature. *Annual Review of Sociology* 37, 55–84.

Small, M. L. (2013). Causal thinking and ethnographic research. *American Journal of Sociology* 119(3), 597–601.

Stake, R. E. (1995). *The art of case study research.* Thousand Oaks, CA: Sage.

Teddlie, C., & Tashakkori, A. (2008). *Foundations of mixed methods research: Integrating qualitative and quantitative approaches in the social and behavioral sciences.* Thousand Oaks, CA: Sage.

Weis, L., Eisenhart, M., & Duncan, G. (2016). *Mixed methods for studies that address road and enduring issues in education research.* Report for Spencer Foundation. Retrieved from http://gse.buffalo.edu/gsefiles/documents/faculty/Mixed-Methods-Statement.pdf.

Yin, R. (2002). *Case study research.* Thousand Oaks, CA: Sage.

Yin, R. (2014). *Case study research* (5th ed.). Thousand Oaks, CA: Sage.

Index

multiple case study 35
multiplicity of variables 29–30

Nadai, E. 12
neo-positivism 28, 31
nested comparison 52, 54
Noah, H. 17

observation 57–60; diversification 59;
 fieldnotes 59; full participation 58;
 observation tools 58; overfamiliarity
 59–60; participant observation 58;
 planning 59; reflexive questions 59;
 reviewing 59; sampling 58
Oke, N. 14
oral histories 95–6
Ortner, S. 9

participant observation 58
Patton, M. 55–6, 118
phenomena 8; contemporary
 phenomena 29
Philips, D. 18
place 12, 13
policy appropriation 2–3, 5, 40
policy as practice 1, 2; policy formation
 2; policy implementation 2
policyscapes 18, 84
Pope, D. 52
Portelli, A. 96
power and inequality 39, 40
process-oriented approach 7, 38–40;
 comparison 15, 16, 19, 40; emergent
 design 38, 39; perspectives of social
 actors 39
purposive sampling 117–18

qualitative surveys 99
quantitative surveys 98, 99
quintain 35

Ragin, C. 16, 27, 29, 116, 122
reliability 32
replication 31
Robertson, S. 3, 14
Roseberry, W. 9

Saldana, J. 100
sampling 52, 55, 58; convenience
 sampling 55; purposive sampling
 117–18; snowball sampling 55
Sampson, R. 101, 102
Sandelowski, M. 123

scale 13–14
Schweisfurth, M. 18
secondary sources 125
Seidman, I. 56
Sheehy, M. 12
Shostak, M. 94
Small, M. 119, 120, 122
snowball sampling 55
social field 12, 52, 115–16
social science research: value of case
 studies 31
space 12, 13; "spatial turn" 44
Stake, R. 30, 33, 34, 35, 115
Steiner-Khamsi, G. 18
Street, B. 10, 38, 122
surveying 98–9

team research 124–5
three axes of comparative research 3;
 horizontal axis 3; overlap of the three
 axes 6; transversal axis 3; vertical axis 3;
 see also horizontal comparison;
 transversal comparison; vertical
 comparison
Tobin, J. 17
tracing 43, 44, 45, 47, 52
"translocal" 43
transversal comparison 92, 100, 108–9;
 archival research 96–8; bilingual
 education and Dominican immigrant
 youth 103–4; central assumptions
 93–4; life histories 94–5; mixed
 methods longitudinal studies
 105–8; oral histories 95–6; qualitative
 longitudinal studies 100–103, 104–5;
 secondary schooling in Tanzania
 105–8; surveying 98–9
Trondman, M. 39
trustworthiness 32
Tsing, A. 3, 40, 41, 45

validity 31; contextual validity 11
van der Veer, P. 51
Van Leeuwen, T. 86
Varenne, H. 17
variance-oriented approach 15, 16,
 28, 29; bounding the case 30–31;
 comparison 15, 16; contemporary
 phenomena 29; generalizability 31;
 limitations of 29–32; multiplicity of
 variables 29–30; neo-positivism 28,
 31; notion of context 29; reliability
 32; replication 31; validity 31

Lightning Source UK Ltd.
Milton Keynes UK
UKHW021001300121
377742UK00016B/368